The 1988 Passport Companion

Publisher: William R. Bonner

Editor: Marian Cooper

Editorial Consultant: Elizabeth Philip

Copy Editors: Kathie Peddicord and Brenda Greene

Managing Editor: Kathleen Murphy

Writers: Janet Schamehorn and Bruce Totaro

Interns: Ellen Chang and Michael Meresman

Production Manager: Becky Mangus

Production: Denise Plowman

ISBN 0-945332-06-8

The 1988 Passport Companion

Table of Contents

Introduction

Travel is an art. Amateurs and beginners choose the basic routes: tours, cruises, and the advertised face-value prices of airline tickets. Those with more sophistication launch into travel after a great deal of planning and bargain hunting. The more you travel, the better you get at finding the best prices, the most interesting routes, and the hidden treasures of the world.

In this book, we share the secrets of the worldly wise traveler. For example, if you know airline lingo, you can save as much as 50% on a ticket price. Many airlines have Frequent Flyer programs that can earn you free trips. Purchasing a ticket overseas can result in great savings. And special train, air, and bus passes not only save money, but they also prevent the headaches caused by language problems at foreign ticket counters.

The who, what, when, where, why, and how of travel are covered in this travel manual. How to save money on travel; exotic festivals throughout Europe; what shots you will need to travel to European countries; how to get visas and travel insurance; what to do if something goes wrong during your trip; how to stay healthy; and a myriad of other topics are discussed. This book also supplies a list of sources you can contact for more information.

Keep this convenient, passport-sized book with you when you travel. By the time you get home, it will probably be creased, folded, and manhandled. That's good. We mean for you to use this little book as a constant, faithful, and reliable companion.

Remember, addresses, prices, and dates were valid at the time of publication. But in the travel business, things change rapidly, sometimes overnight. So be sure to check before you leave for your trip.

Please let us know if we have left out any important

information, or if you have any tips of your own that other travelers would appreciate. When the *Passport Companion* is updated, we will include your suggestions.

Have fun planning your next trip. And bon voyage.

—Marian Cooper

Chapter 1

Special Travel Angles

The world of travel is filled with secrets. If you know them, you can save money. You don't have to be rich to see Europe. In fact, you don't even have to be wealthy to travel first-class! Finding the best bargains can be a game. The object is to find the lowest price. And when you win, you win big.

You can fly, take a train, drive, or sail to your destination. If you plan to travel any distance, you probably will fly. So we will begin this chapter with a discussion of air fares and how to find the best bargains.

FLYING HIGH FOR A LOW PRICE

If you know the ins and outs, you can save money on airline tickets. You can book a flight with a charter company—if you know your itinerary months in advance. Or you can wait until the last minute and see which companies are selling leftover tickets at low prices. You can buy first-class seats for half-price through a coupon broker, or you can fly standby. You can purchase tickets at overseas bucket shops or at American discount travel agencies. Or you can buy an Ultra Super Saver ticket from a major airline. Whichever way you decide to go will take a fair amount of thought.

Bargain airlines

The first step when looking for bargain air fares is to compare the prices offered by different airlines. Since deregulation in 1978, competition between airlines has been fierce. Smaller airlines trying to muscle their ways in offer cheap, bare-bones flights. You may have to do without some amenities, but the savings between smaller companies and the major lines can be tremendous.

The trouble with all this competition is that companies often go bankrupt (remember Freddie Laker, Air Florida?). And when they go out of business, other airlines do not always honor their tickets. So you're left holding a worthless ticket. Your best safeguard: Don't hold onto a ticket for more than a couple months.

Bargain airlines also often reduce the space between seats, making for cramped quarters. Sometimes meals are not included in the air fare, and an extra charge is tacked on for baggage.

Still, the savings can be great. And because of the low prices offered by smaller airlines, major companies have been forced to lower their ticket prices somewhat, too. Major airlines usually are willing to match the price of a low-cost airline if you make your reservation in advance.

Following is a list of some of the bargain airlines that fly to Europe: Braniff, Continental, Icelandair, Lufthansa, and Virgin Atlantic.

Discount agencies

The best way to research fares is to decide your destination as early as possible, then pay careful attention to airline advertisements. Travel discounters and wholesalers offer great bargains. Their ads are often tiny, so read even the smallest ones. These agencies sell a large volume of tickets at low prices and make their profits from extra commissions and bonuses. For tickets that cost less than $300 and for heavily traveled routes, significant discounts probably are not available.

These discount agencies sell tickets on major airlines for a lower rate than the airlines themselves. This is usually done with the blessing of the airline, believe it or not. The airline wants to fill empty seats this way on under-traveled routes or during off-seasons.

For example, **TFI Tours International** of New York, *(212) 736-1140,* and **Unitravel** of St. Louis offer discount rates on carriers that cross the Atlantic. **TFI Tours International** (one of the biggest discount agents) recently offered a round-trip fare between New York and London for $276. **Up and Away Travel** of New York sells tickets aboard Air-India from New York to

London for more than $100 less than the official rate.

But use caution when buying from discounters. You could be stuck flying a prolonged, roundabout route. And your homeward flight could be subject to change.

If you are unsure of an agency, check with the Better Business Bureau or your local consumer affairs department before purchasing a ticket.

Following is a list of travel agencies that specialize in bargain air fares and tours:

- **Access International**, *(800)223-1580 or (212)333-7280 in New York.*
- **Charles Aris**, *(212)734-0051.*
- **HTI Tours**, *(800)441-6484 or (215)592-7300 in Philadelphia.*
- **TFI Tours International Ltd.**, *(800)223-6363 or (212)736-1140 in New York.*
- **Ticket & Tours**, *(800)826-6046 or (212)697-7895 in New York.*
- **Travel Discounts International**, *(212)826-6644.*
- **Up and Away Travel Inc.**, *(212)972-2345.*

Ultra Super Saver fares

Ultra Super Saver fares, which must be bought 30 days in advance and have a cancellation penalty of 25%, are usually the cheapest fares advertised by airlines. While these fares can save you up to 75%, your ticket may not be transferable to another airline. And if you miss your flight, you will face a stiff penalty of 25% to 50% of your ticket price when you ask for a refund.

Advance Purchase Excursion (APEX) fares are also inexpensive. These must be purchased 14 to 30 days ahead of time and usually require that you stay at your destination for at least a week. Some of these bargain fares are non-refundable, which has caused an uproar among consumers. But a few travel agents and airlines will guarantee to refund tickets. Shop around.

Flying standby

One of the cheapest ways to fly—if you don't mind waiting around in an airport for hours—is with a standby ticket. These tickets are very inexpensive, but you have to wait until a seat is available on an airplane. Avoid holidays and weekends, when airports are packed. The best times to travel standby are during the week, at night, and during your destination's off-season.

Taking a chance on charters

Charter flights are often good deals. The operators arrange flights (and hotels) between heavily traveled routes. By moving large numbers of travelers every week, the operators are able to get huge price reductions, which they pass on to customers. But you must get to the departure city on your own. If you cancel after you have paid, you usually lose the full price of the flight. Most companies advertise a base price, add a fee (usually 15% of the base figure), and then tack on a surcharge. It can be very difficult to find the actual total cost, even for travel agents. If you are traveling alone, most charter companies also charge a few hundred dollars extra as a single supplement.

If you choose this route, pay with a credit card. This protects you from losing your money if the charter company goes out of business, as they often do. Operators can cancel a charter up to 10 days before departure. And the flight time and date can be changed any time. Tour operators can increase the price as much as 10% up to 10 days before departure. If you miss your plane, you can't catch the next one out, because these are not regularly scheduled flights. So DON'T miss that plane!

With some quick telephone research you can check out an agent's reputation through organizations such as the **American Society of Travel Agents**. The society requires its members to have been in business for at least three years. It doesn't keep a list of bad guys, but by contacting the society's *Office of Consumer Affairs, 4400 MacArthur Blvd. N.W., Washington, DC 20007; (202)965-7520,* you can find out how long member agencies have been in business and get a history of complaints.

Another organization that requires its members to maintain a certain level of competence and financial stability is the **Association of Retail Travel Agents**, *25 S. Riverside, P.O. Box 388, Croton-on-Hudson, NY 10520; (914)271-4357.*

One especially inexpensive charter organization is **International Weekends' Charter Vacations Inc.,** *(617)449-5450.* This organization recently advertised an around-the-world tour with stops in London, Paris, Rome, India, Hong Kong, and Tokyo, including air fare and hotels, for $2,599.

Frequent Flyers and coupon brokers

Business travelers can get free flights by signing up with an airline that has a Frequent Flyer program. These arrangements allow travelers to accumulate points toward a free flight each time they fly. Free hotel rooms, cruises, and auto rentals are sometimes included in these programs, too.

Coupon brokers buy these Frequent Flyer awards and resell them to the public and to travel agents at low prices. Coupons are especially good deals if you fly first- or business-class, or if you fly very long distances. Generally, you must wait five to six weeks to get the coupon issued in your name.

Following is a list of some coupon brokers:

- **AGCO**, *(800)872-2426, (212)529-5555 in New York,* or *(213)459-0404 in Los Angeles.*
- **Air Line Coupon Company**, *(800)338-0099* or *(800)345-4489.*
- **American Coupon Exchange**, *(714)644-4112.*
- **Frequent Flyer, Ltd.**, *(617)742-0072.*
- **International Air Coupon Exchange**, *(800)558-0053.*
- **Nesher Travel**, *(800)343-4070.*
- **Premier Travel**, *(800)4-AIRTIX* or *(619)275-6314 in San Diego.*
- **Pricebusters**, *(800)424-7849.*
- **The Coupon Broker**, *(303)759-1953.*
- **The Coupon Bank**, *(800)292 9250.*
- **The Flyer's Edge**, *(312)256-8200.*
- **The Horizon Group**, *(800)4-Flyers.*
- **Travel Deluxe International**, *(212)826-6644, (312)922-3888,* or *(818)845-3322.*
- **Travel Discounts International**, *(212)826-6644* or *(312)922-3808.*
- **Travel Mart**, *(800)443-CASH* or *(214)750-7600 in Dallas.*

For more information on Frequent Flyer programs and coupon brokers, read *The Frequent Flyer Guide* by Kriss Hammond. To

order a copy, send $6.95 plus $1.50 for postage and handling to
1988 Guide, *1220 Third St., Spearfish, SD 57783.*

The ABCs of alphabet fares

Alphabet fares, which aren't advertised by airlines, are one of
the best-kept travel secrets. These fares are often much lower than
the lowest prices advertised and are used mainly by airline
employees and people in the travel industry. If you know the
airline lingo, you can save as much as 50% on ticket prices.

You must ask for alphabet fares—airlines won't volunteer the
information. And not all airlines use the same letters. But you can
guess at the terminology using the following guidelines. Generally, a Y fare means unrestricted coach. YN is unrestricted coach
on a night flight. M and B fares are both cheaper than Y but are
limited to a certain number of seats on each flight (they have other
restrictions as well). H or Q means coach economy discounted.
QN is a night coach economy discounted. L or V is thrift
discounted. K is thrift. OFPK is off-peak. Q, K, and V fares are
usually promotional and only valid for a limited time. Go ahead
and take a shot at it. Pick up the phone, call an airline, and ask for
a K fare to your favorite destination. If you're lucky, you'll end up
with the cheapest rate. If the person at the other end of the line
acts like you're crazy, hang up and call back later. Ask for an M
fare. After all, you've got nothing to lose.

Bucket shops

Enormous discounts (up to two-thirds off) are not unusual on
tickets sold by overseas discount travel agencies, known as bucket
shops. Low overhead and high-volume sales keep prices low.
Generally, shops are small, with a few travel posters on the walls
and a few pieces of furniture. The best locations for these bargain
shops are London, Athens, Amsterdam, Singapore, Bangkok, and
Hong Kong. Although they sell scheduled flights with the major
airlines, the very cheapest flights are with less-known (often Third
World) airlines or Eastern bloc airlines, such as the Russian
carrier Aeroflot.

But these flights have their disadvantages. Shops are not
always licensed and bonded. Also, you might want to avoid flying

on crafts of small airlines from Third-World countries, because safety standards may be less than adequate. Be cautious when dealing with bucket shops. Cancellation penalties are high. Also, if the agency is not a member of the International Air Transport Association (IATA), you may not have any recourse if you get a bad ticket (paying by credit card can be a safeguard). Stick with companies that have been in business for a few years.

In London. London bucket shops are famous for having incredibly low prices. But that notoriety may be unfounded these days. "A couple years ago, when the almighty dollar truly merited that name, you could book some of the best bargains from bucket shops in London," wrote Editor Bruce Totaro in the April 1987 issue of **Travel Savings Hotline**, *824 E. Baltimore St., Baltimore, MD 21212.* "At that time, those cut-rate purveyors offered very low fares between the United States and Europe. With today's weaker dollar, the London discounters no longer head the bargain brigade. In fact, tickets purchased from U.S.-based discounters are often better buys." Totaro compared prices offered by London bucket shops and New York-based discounters and found that the New York fares are lower in general.

London bucket shops are also losing ground to larger, more established agencies that have gotten into the field of discount tickets. While you may have to request the low fares specifically, these agencies provide more security than bucket shops.

London bucket shops are advertised in *Time Out* magazine, *LAM*, and the *Evening Standard*. The following bucket shops take major credit cards and will send tickets to you in the United States:

• **Bestways Travel and Tours Ltd.**, *56/58 Whitcomb St., London WC2; tel. (44-1)930-1992.* This company has been around for 14 years and is good.

• **Worldwide Cheap Travel**, *254 Earls Court Road, London SW5.*

• **InterAtlas Travel**, *11 Madox St., London W1R 90A; tel. (44-1)493-0071.*

• **Latitude 40**, *13 Beauchamp Place, London SW3 1NQ; tel. (44-1)581-1861.*

In Amsterdam. In Amsterdam you can find some of the cheapest long-haul tickets in all Europe. Look for bucket shops on streets such as Rokin and Damstraat, off Dam Square. You'll also find bargains in the Montplein area. Two shops on Rokin Street are **Holland International Travel Group**, *tel. (31-20)264-466,* and **Near East Tours**, *tel. (31-20)243-350.*

In Athens. Travel firms offering surprising bargains can be found on and around Fillelinon and Wikis streets, off Syntagma Square. **Egnatia**, *Fillelinon 7,* often has good deals. **Transalpino**, *Nikis 28,* is another good bet.

In Frankfurt. Ads for bucket shops can be found in the "Reisewelt" section of *Welt am Sonntag (Sunday World)* and in the *Frankfurter Allgemeine* or *Suddeutscher Zeitung.*

Currency fluctuations and cross-border ticketing

Currency fluctuations can save you money on airline tickets. You are ahead of the game if you can buy both halves of a round-trip ticket in a country where the exchange rate is in your favor. You can accomplish this by having a foreign contact buy your ticket for you overseas. When your ticket arrives in the United States, you simply use the second coupon—from the United States to the given country—first.

If you are flying one-way but can get a better deal on a round-trip ticket, sell the second half of your ticket to someone else. Although airlines like to charge extra to change the traveler's name on a ticket, they usually won't say anything if it looks like the person who sold the ticket made an error. Less scrupulous people type in their own names with the help of red carbon paper. The airlines and the law in most countries take a dim view of this practice.

Tickets are cheaper in some European countries than in others. Amsterdam is probably the least expensive place in Europe to buy a long-haul airline ticket these days, so many non-Dutch passengers purchase tickets there. But you don't have to go to Amsterdam for a ticket. If you're in London and going to Singapore, for instance, the travel agent issues a ticket from Amsterdam to London to Singapore and back via London. At the end of your trip, you return to London and still have a London-to-Amsterdam flight coupon, valid for up to a year. The savings can be considerable.

The virtues of getting bumped

When airlines overbook, they have to bump passengers. At first glance, this is a disaster. Actually, though, it can be a blessing. Passengers who are bumped often get to fly for free on the next flight out! If you find yourself in line for an overbooked flight, volunteer to be bumped. It isn't difficult to guess which flights might be oversold. Good candidates are flights leaving on Friday evenings from major business centers and flights during busy holidays.

For more information on discount flights

If you want to dig up your own information on airline routes and prices, consult the ***Official Airline Guide*** (OAG); the ***Airfare Discount Bulletin*** (ADB), *P.O. Box 460, Riverside, CT 06878;* or ***Travel Marketing Magazine***, *Jet Transport Exchange Inc., 280 Tokeneke Road, Darien, CT 06820.* ***Travel Savings Hotline*** (TSH), *Agora Publishing, 824 E. Baltimore St., Baltimore, MD 21202; (301)234-0515*, also lists current travel bargains. The good deals TSH has reported include a round-trip air fare from New York to Paris for $250.

TO CLUB OR NOT TO CLUB

Travel clubs are mushrooming these days. They offer bargain rates (as much as 50% off) on tours, charters, cruises, and airlines. Members get information on bargains through a newsletter or a telephone hotline, then choose trips convenient to them. Membership fees generally are not high—they range from $25 to $100 per year. However, clubs are worth the membership fee only if you travel frequently and the bargains coincide with your schedule. Look into a club carefully before you join—scams abound. Find out if the club operates on a regional, a national, or an international basis. Following is a list of some of the major travel clubs, along with the membership fee for each:

- **ADCI/Club Costa**, *(800)225-0381*, $99.
- **Adventures on Call**, *(301)356-4080*, $49.
- **Airhitch/Worldwide Destinations Unlimited**, *(212)864-2000*, $25.
- **American Travel Association**, *(800)553-8500*, $39.
- **Discount Travel International**, *(215)668-2182*, $45.
- **Encore**, *(800)638-8976*, $48.
- **First Travel Club**, *(312)240-2626*, $48.
- **Impulse**, *(800)251-8853* or *(303)740-8700 in Colorado*, $75.
- **Last Minute Travel Club**, *(617)267-9800*, $30.
- **Moment's Notice**, *(212)486-0503* or *(206)453-1180*, $45.
- **Short Notice Go-Card**, *(800)638-8976*, $36.
- **Stand-Buys, Ltd.**, *(800)621-5839*, $45.
- **Travel Discounts Unlimited**, *(303)420-6807*, $45.
- **Worldwide Discount Travel Club**, *(305)534-2082*, $35 to $50.

For more information, read *The Travel and Vacation Discount Guide*, available for $3.95 plus $1 postage and handling from **Pilot Books**, *103 Cooper St., Babylon, NY 11702; (212)685-0736.*

BARGAIN FARES FOR SPECIAL GROUPS

Senior citizens, young people, singles, and the disabled will find that a number of discount rates and special deals apply to them when traveling. Rather than being limited, these groups are in many ways privileged when it comes to travel.

Senior citizens

A number of travel clubs cater to senior citizens, offering them discount rates on hotels and transportation. One of the best is Elderhostel, which arranges study tours for travelers over 60. Tours include learning the art of French cooking at an 18th-century chateau near Paris. Participants stay in dormitories while they take the courses, which cost about $205 a person, not including transportation.

A 64-page catalog lists more than 20,000 educational opportunities in Great Britain, Australia, Scandinavia, and other European countries. For more information, contact **Elderhostel**, *80 Boylston St., Suite 400, Boston, MA 02116; (617)426-8056.*

Youth programs

Students have the world at their fingertips. Throughout Europe, student IDs qualify travelers for discounts on transportation, entry fees to museums and movies, and other attractions. And youth hostels provide inexpensive and clean places to stay. Below are some of the organizations that provide inexpensive travel services to students and young people:

• **American International Student Exchange**, *7728 Lookout Dr., La Jolla, CA 92037; (619)459-9761.*

• **American Youth Hostels**, *P.O. Box 37613, Washington, DC 20013-7613; (202)783-6161.* These are open to everyone regardless of age.

• **Antioch International**, *79 Livermore St., Yellow Springs, OH 45387; (513)767-1031.* This group arranges study tours in Europe.

• **Canadian Hostelling Association**, *333 River Road, Vanier City, Ottawa, K1L 8B9 Canada.* All ages can participate.

• **Council for International Educational Exchange** (CIEE), *205 E. 42nd St., New York, NY 10017; (212)661-1414.* This youth travel agency helps students find employment overseas.

• **Education Foundation for Foreign Study**, *1528 Chapala St., Santa Barbara, CA 93101; (805)963-0553.* Study abroad and homestays are arranged.

• **International Christian Youth Exchange**, *134 W. 26th St., New York, NY 10001; (212)206-7307.* This group arranges international exchange programs.

• **NACEL Cultural Exchanges**, *130 N. Terrace, Fargo, ND 58102; (701)232-8800.* This organization sponsors educational programs and homestays abroad.

• **Open Door Student Exchange**, *124 E. Merrick Road, Valley Stream, NY 11580; (516)825-8485.* This group specializes in exchange programs for students 15 to 18 that last from three to six months.

• **United States Student Travel Service**, *801 Second Ave., Suite 1501, New York, NY 10017; (212)867-8770.* This group offers travel services, homestays, study programs, cheap flights, tours, and summer jobs for travelers of all ages.

• **Youth Exchange Services, Inc.,** *World Trade Center, 350 S. Figueroa St., Los Angeles, CA 90071; (800)848-2121.* Study programs and homestays are arranged.

• **Youth for Understanding**, *3501 Newark St. N.W., Washington, DC 20016; (202)966-6800.* This organization works with the Department of State to arrange international exchange programs for teenagers.

Singles

Traveling alone can be lonely if you aren't the gregarious type. If you are single, you can join travel groups that cater to fellow singles. Prices are lower because you don't pay the single supplement usually charged for a room or berth. And you will be introduced to new people.

Tour companies that cater to singles include:

• **Single Tour Company**, *P.O. Box 5107, Redondo, WA 98054; (206)941-6413.*

• **Travel Companion Exchange, Inc.,** *P.O. Box 833, Amityville, NY 11701; (516)454-0880.* This computerized service matches single travelers.

• **Travel Mates, Inc.,** *49 W. 44th St., New York, NY 10036; (212)221-6565.*

• **Travel Partners Club**, *P.O. Box 2368, Crystal River, FL 32629; (904)795-1117.*

Disabled travelers

Many train and airline systems offer reduced fares for the disabled. And several organizations provide information and tips to handicapped travelers. Following is a list of tour operators and other services that can help handicapped travelers:

• **Access to the World**, *2828 E. Colfax Ave., Denver, CO 80206,* is a tour operator specializing in international travel for the disabled.

• **Flying Wheels Travel**, *143 W. Bridge, Owatonna, MN 55060,* is a tour operator for the handicapped.

• *The Itinerary*, *P.O. Box 1084, Bayonne, NJ 07002,* is a magazine for handicapped travelers.

- ***LTD Travel**, 116 Harbor Seal Court, San Mateo, CA 94404*, is a
newsletter for disabled travelers.
- **Mobility International U.S.A.**, *P.O. Box 3551, Eugene, OR
97403*, is an information service for handicapped travelers.
- **Moss Rehabilitation Hospital Travel Information Center**, *12
Tabor Road, Philadelphia, PA 19141*, offers travel information
for the disabled.
- **Wheels on Tour, Inc.**, *20202 Cohasset, Canoga Park, CA
91306,* is a tour operator that specializes in international travel for
people confined to wheelchairs.
- **Whole Person Tours**, *P.O. Box 1084, Bayonne, NJ 07002,*
offers tours for the disabled.

TRAVELING BY FREIGHTER

Travelers who can't abide the thought of soaring through thin
air hundreds of miles above the earth may prefer crossing the
ocean by freighter. While freighter travel is more expensive and
slower than flying, the food is usually excellent, and you have
your own comfortable stateroom rather than a cramped airplane
seat. Freighters usually take only about a dozen passengers.

According to Ed Kirk, president of TravLtips Cruise and
Freighter Travel Service, freighter travel is gaining popularity.
Several shipping lines recently have initiated passenger service on
their cargo ships, and more are planning to take on passengers.

TravLtips is a great source of information on freighter travel in
general. Members of the association receive *TravLtips Magazine*,
which contains firsthand accounts of cruise experiences as well as
current fares and schedules; the services of the association's
reservation department; and invitations to join special group
cruises. Memberships are $30 per year.

The freighter lines that can be booked through TravLtips
include Lykes and Cast. Lykes sails to South America, the Far
East, Africa, the Mediterranean, Europe, and the Gulf of Mexico.
Prices start at $1,500 one-way for the eight-day European
crossing.

Cast sails from Montreal to Antwerp, Belgium. The Atlantic
crossing takes about 12 days. The ship docks in Antwerp for about

a week while cargo is unloaded (passengers can come and go as they please). The round-trip cruise takes about 32 days. Staterooms have air conditioning and private bathrooms. The cost is $3,150 round trip, $1,575 one way.

Two other agents that specialize in freighter travel are **Air and Marine Travel Service**, *501 Madison Ave., New York, NY 10022; (212)371-1300*, and **Pearl's Travel Tips**, *175 Great Neck Road, Suite 306, Great Neck, NY 11024; (516)487-8351* or *(212)895-7656*.

GETTING AROUND IN A FOREIGN COUNTRY

Travel throughout your destination country need not be expensive or uncomfortable. Air and train travel passes, for example, can save you money. And, if you're planning a relatively short stay, renting a car can be a good way to see the countryside at your leisure.

Travel passes

Air travel passes allow multiple stops, unlimited flights, and discounts on flights within various countries. Most air passes must be purchased outside the country where you wish to travel. Some require that you arrive on the national carrier of the destination country.

For example, **Finnair's Holiday Ticket** is good for 15 days of travel all over Finland and costs $250. The **Youth Holiday Ticket** is $200. Passes can be purchased at Finnair offices.

Iberia's Visit Spain Airpass is good for 60 days and allows one stop in each city. It costs $199 (add $50 to include the Canary Islands).

Train passes

Every summer thousands of American students descend upon Europe with **Eurailpass** in hand. It is the best known and most popular travel pass and allows unlimited train travel throughout most of Europe for a specified amount of time. It is good for travel on the national railroads of 16 European countries, as well as passage on some ferries and steamers and discounts on many private railroads, buses, and ferries. All the West European countries except Great Britain accept the Eurailpass.

For first-class travel, prices are $280 for 15 days; $350 for 21 days; $440 for one month; $620 for two months; and $760 for three months. Travelers under 26 can purchase a second-class Eurailpass for $310 for one month; $400 for two months.

To get a Eurailpass, contact **European Rail**, *918 16th St. N.W., Washington, DC 20006; (202)659-9581*. The pass must be purchased in North America before departure.

A number of other train passes also can save you money if you plan to do a lot of traveling in a certain region.

The **BritRail Pass**, for example, permits unlimited travel in England, Wales, and Scotland. An eight-day ticket costs $149 economy-class, $210 first-class; a 15-day ticket costs $225 economy-class, $315 first-class; a 22-day ticket costs $285 economy-class, $400 first-class; and a month-long ticket is $335 economy-class, $470 first-class.

A **Senior Citizen BritRail** allows first-class travel for only slightly more than economy rates. Passes must be bought in the United States before you leave for England. They can be pur-chased through any travel agent or from **BritRail**, *630 Third Ave., New York, NY 10017*.

A **Scottish Highland Travelpass**, also available from BritRail, allows unlimited travel on trains, buses, and ferries in the Scottish Highlands. From March to May, a 14-day pass costs $75. From June to September, a 7-day pass costs $72, and a 14-day pass costs $110.

A **Rambler Pass** allows unlimited travel in Ireland, and tickets can be bought at any bus or train station there. Rail- or bus only passes are available for 8 days for $66; 15-day passes are $98. Passes allowing unlimited travel on trains and buses are $84 for 8 days, $122 for 15 days. Children under 16 pay half-fare.

An **Overlander Pass** provides unlimited bus and train travel in Ireland and Northern Ireland for 15 days for $139. Both the Rambler Pass and the Overlander Pass are available from **CIE Tours International**, *122 E. 42nd St., New York, NY 10168; (800)CIE-TOUR or (212)972-5600*.

France's **Vacances Pass** entitles you to unlimited travel on the

French national railroads. In addition, it includes a Metropass for four to seven days of travel on the Paris subways and buses; round-trip airport transfers; a free trip on the private Provence railroad between Digne and Nice; a $10 discount on bus excursions sponsored by the French national railroad; and free entry to the Pompidou Museum. Four-day tickets are $89 first-class, $69 second-class; 9-day tickets are $190 first-class, $130 second-class; and 16-day tickets are $250 first-class, $170 second-class. They are available from your travel agent or the **French National Railroads**, *610 Fifth Ave., New York, NY 10020; (212)582-2110.*

A **Finnrailpass** is good for unlimited travel on all trains in Finland. The 8-day pass is $120 first-class, $80 second-class; the 15-day pass is $171 first-class, $114 second-class; and the 22-day pass is $219 first-class, $146 second-class. Children under 12 get a 50% discount. Groups of three or more get a 20% discount. The pass can be purchased at railway stations in Finland; through **Holiday Tours of America**, *40 E. 49th St., New York, NY 10017; (212)832-9072 or (800)233-0567;* or through **Scantours**, *1535 Sixth St., Santa Monica, CA 90401; (213)451-0911 or (800)223-SCAN.*

The **Belgium Rail Pass** allows unlimited first-class train travel within Belgium for 5 days for $56 or for 16 days for $105. Unlimited second-class travel is $37 for 5 days; $70 for 16 days. A half-fare card, good for one month, gives a 50% discount on train travel for children between the ages of 12 and 18. It costs $10.50 first-class, $7 second-class. The card must be purchased from Belgium Rail in Belgium.

Spain offers a tourist card that allows 8 days of unlimited train travel for $100 first-class, $75 second-class; a 15-day card for $160 first-class, $120 second-class; and a 22-day card for $200 first-class, $160 second-class. The pass can be purchased at any Spanish train station.

The **Italian Tourist Ticket,** also known as the BTLC, provides 8 days of unlimited travel for $134 first-class, $85 second-class; 15 days for $164 first-class, $103 second-class; 21 days for $195 first-class, $120 second-class; and one month for $238 first-class, $150 second-class. The pass can be purchased at the **Italian State**

Railroad Office, *666 Fifth Ave., Sixth Floor, New York, NY 10103; (212)397-2667.*

A **German Rail Tourist Card** provides unlimited travel. The 4-day pass is $110 first-class, $75 second-class; the 9-day pass is $170 first-class, $115 second-class; and the 16-day pass is $230 first-class, $160 second-class. The card can be bought at German train stations.

A **Swiss Holiday Card** also offers unlimited travel. The 4-day pass is $120 first-class, $80 second-class; the 8-day pass is $140 first-class, $95 second-class; the 15-day pass is $165 first-class, $115 second-class; and the month-long pass is $235 first-class, $160 second-class. Swiss train stations sell the card.

A **Scandinavian Rail Pass**, good for 21 days of travel in Finland, Sweden, Norway, and Denmark, costs $280 first-class, $187 second-class. The pass can be bought at any train station in any of the countries it covers.

Driving

Driving gives you a flexibility that you won't find if you travel by bus or train. Small towns and country areas that are not accessible otherwise are available for your exploration. And you don't have to set your clock for 5 a.m. to make the only train to Zurich, for instance. You can drive there after a leisurely breakfast and a shower!

On the other hand, driving in another country can be hazardous. If you can fathom the depths of Roman driving customs, you probably qualify for the Indianapolis 500!

Driving in Europe and most other areas of the world is much more expensive than in the United States—gas prices in Europe are almost double those in the United States.

This may explain why mass transit systems are so efficient overseas. In most cases, you don't really need a car. Trains and subways go almost everywhere. Before you decide to rent a car and take off, read up on local laws. Learn what the signs mean. Make sure you have the proper papers and insurance. You don't want to end up in jail somewhere because you didn't have the right papers. Car rental companies or the American Automobile

Association (AAA) can give you information.

Before driving in Europe, read *AA Motoring in Europe*, edited by Patricia Kelly. It's available from the Automobile Association in Hampshire, England. It includes information on driving laws, parking, maps, and road signs.

A valid driver's license is required to drive in Europe. Your U.S. license is sufficient in most countries except Spain, which also requires bail bond. But it's a good idea to get an **International Driving Permit** (IDP), which translates your license into foreign languages and will save you grief if you ever tangle with the police. To get one, contact AAA. You fill out an application, present your American driver's license and a passport photo, and pay $5. (Even if you do get an IDP, you still need your American license to drive in Europe.)

Do not drive in Europe without insurance. Your American car insurance won't cover you there, and you must buy insurance that will. You can purchase insurance from banks and European insurance companies.

To drive across European borders you need the **Green Card**—an all-risk insurance that protects you against everything. It can be purchased from European insurance companies and banks. If you plan to stay in one country, you can buy limited protection insurance.

Car rental companies will sell you insurance that covers driving abroad. So will AAA. European insurance is twice as expensive as American. But if you have a good driving record and no claims on your American policy, you may be able to get a policy for 40% off. Before you leave the United States, get a letter from your insurance agent stating that you have driven for the past four years without making a claim. This entitles you to a "no-claims bonus," which can cut your insurance costs.

Renting a car

Your travel agent or AAA can help you find a car rental agency. Hertz, Avis, National, and Budget all have offices in the major cities. These companies will send you lists of their locations, rates, taxes, and insurance requirements.

European car rental agencies are sometimes cheaper than those in the United States. The national tourist agency of the country where you plan to travel can give you information. Cars of all sizes and prices are available. Gas is never included in the price, but you can get a car with unlimited mileage. Europe by Car, Inc. is an organization that can help you buy, lease, or rent a car in Europe. For example, a Volkswagon Fox or Panda (a hatchback) can be rented in Germany for 14 days for $178, with unlimited mileage. Or you can rent a Porsche 944 for seven days for $169. For more information, contact **Europe by Car Inc.**, *One Rockefeller Plaza, New York, NY 10020; (212)581-3040*, or *9000 Sunset Blvd., Los Angeles, CA 90069; (213)272-0424.*

Buying can be better

Renting a car can be expensive if you are traveling for longer than a week or two. The alternative is to buy one and then sell it when you are ready to leave. This is easy to arrange. You can either buy your car directly from the manufacturer or from a dealer.

Renault, for instance, has a purchase/repurchase vacation plan that costs less than renting a car. There are two plans: the 23-day plan is $30.22 a day, including insurance; the 47-day plan is $19.68 a day, including insurance. One benefit of the program is that it's sales tax-free. If you pick up and return the cars in Paris or Nice, no delivery or return fees are charged. In the long run, this is cheaper than renting a car at the going rate of $23.74 a day, plus insurance and turnover taxes! Orders should be placed at least four weeks before delivery. For more information, contact **Renault's European Delivery Services**, *650 First Ave., New York, NY 10016; (800)221-1052* or *(212)532-1221.*

Europe Auto Brokers Inc., *P.O. Box 214, 3430-AE Nieuwegein-N, Netherlands; tel. (34)024-1346,* sells European cars duty- and tax-free directly from the factory to the public. Delivery time for high-performance models, such as Mercedes Benz and Rolls Royce, is three to five months. For other makes, delivery time is 8 to 14 weeks.

If you prefer to buy in person through a car dealership, London is the logical place to begin your shopping. Many flights to Europe land there, and the language is familiar. It is easier and cheaper to shop in small towns outside London. British news agents sell monthly car booklets that list the prices you can expect to pay. Find a car dealer (look in the Yellow Pages of the local telephone book) who will agree to repurchase the car when your trip is over—for a slight but fair profit to himself of perhaps 10%. British cars are the best buys. Non-British cars are expensive in Britain because of the high import duties.

Once you have made your purchase, the dealer will handle the paper work. All you need to do is find an insurance agent. There are plenty of independent agents to choose from, and most deal with General Accident Assurance Corp., Ltd., which covers foreigners seeking either temporary or permanent insurance.

A few driving tips

Drivers are aggressive and fast in most of Europe (except in Scandinavia, where they are usually polite). For the most part, European motorists use their horns heavily and ignore intersections. Following is a list of tips to keep in mind when making your way along European highways.

• In Europe, it is illegal to pass on the right. It is also illegal to drive in the left lane of an expressway, except to pass another car.

• The autobahn in Germany has no speed limit, and drivers often go 125 mph. Keep to the right!

• In Britain and Ireland, drive on the left side of the road—not the right.

• In Portugal, drivers honk at curves on mountain roads to warn oncoming vehicles.

• In Sweden, you must turn on your headlights any time you drive, day or night. Also, Swedes and Spaniards pull over onto the shoulder to let faster cars pass.

• Drinking and driving is seriously punished in Europe. You can be stopped and tested at any time.

• In Holland, radar cameras are mounted on the sides of roads.

They photograph speeders. Police then trace the license plate number and send the car's owner a ticket. These devices are also used at traffic lights.

• Between stop lights in many German cities, there are posts with lighted numbers that indicate the maximum speed you can drive to avoid stopping at the next red light.

• Children under 10 may not ride in the front seat in most European countries (in countries where they can ride in the front seat, they must wear special seat belts).

• Gas stations usually keep regular business hours. Don't expect to find one open on Sunday or late at night. Keep your tank full.

• Seatbelts are required when driving in Europe.

TRAVELING WITH A TOUR

Traveling independently can be a tiring and inefficient way to visit an area of Europe you know nothing about. For this reason, many travelers turn to tours. An organized tour takes care of travel arrangements, hotels, language problems, cultural differences, and sometimes food.

The trouble with tours is that they have to be just right, or they're horrible. No one wants to be stuck for several weeks with a tour group and guide he dislikes, an itinerary he wouldn't choose for himself, and accommodations that don't suit his style.

Sample tours

The culinary secrets of Burgundy and the finest wines of France are sampled on the French tour sponsored by **Society Expeditions**, *3131 Elliott Ave., Suite 700, Seattle, WA 98121; (800)426-7794*. Stay in a 16th-century inn and dine at Chez Camille, located in Arnay-le-Duc. Master Chef Armand Poinsot and his wife, Monique, give lessons in French cuisine. The eight-day tour starts at $2,190.

Bacchants' Pilgrimages, *101 Roundtree Blvd., P.O. Box 12732, San Rafael, CA 94913-2732; (415)479-9698*, sponsors one-week, do-it-yourself wine tours of France. Included are rental cars, hotel accommodations, meals, copies of *Guide to Visiting Vineyards with Bacchants' Pilgrimages, The Marling Menu*

Master for France, French Country Inns and Chateau Hotels, and Michelin maps and *Green Guides*. The prices range from $300 per person to $945 per person.

Europeds, *883 Sinex Ave., Pacific Grove, CA 93950; (408)372-1173*, offers 11 bike and 4 hiking tours of Europe. One of the most interesting itineraries is a Swiss hut-hopping hike through the Alps from Lucerne to St. Moritz. The nine-day tour spans two separate Alpine regions and crosses mountains, valleys, and glaciers. The cost is $1,195.

Butterfield and Robinson, *70 Bond St., Toronto, Ontario, Canada M5B 1X3; (416)864-1354*, leads biking and hiking tours through Europe that are far from "roughing it." Participants stay in villas, castles, and country homes. And the food and wine are superb. Routes are designed for casual bikers who want to enjoy Europe at a leisurely pace. The daily distance traveled is about 30 miles. The route through Alsace takes a week and costs $1,595.

Maupintour, *P.O. Box 807, Lawrence, KS 66044; (800)255-4266*, also offers European tours. Itineraries are comprehensive and include Austria/Bavaria, the British Isles, Greece, Italy, the Netherlands, Scandinavia, Spain, Switzerland, and all Europe.

Travellers International Tour Operators offers "Viking Vacations" in conjunction with SAS (Scandinavian Airline System). The "Viking Adventure" tour, which costs $789 to $869, not including air fare, visits Oslo and the Norwegian lakes, cruises the fjords, follows the banks of Lusterfjord, and takes you through the countryside of Dalarna, Sweden, Stockholm, Sweden's Lake District, and Copenhagen. For information, contact **SAS**, *138-02 Queens Blvd., Jamaica, NY 11435; (800)221-2350* or *(718)657-7700*.

Iberia Airlines, *(800)2221-9741*, offers a "Fly/Drive" tour to Spain that includes round-trip air fare and a rental car for a week. The price is $594 to $652.

If you don't mind touring by bus, **Globus Gateway**, *95-25 Queen's Blvd., Rego Park, NY 11374; (800)221-0090* in the eastern United States, *(718)268-7000* in New York, and *(800)556-5454* in the western United States, offers extensive bus tours of Europe. Just about anywhere you want to go in Europe is visited by Globus Gateway. Most hotels en route are first-class. Tours include: "Britain Sampler" ($299 to $389, not including air fare); "Emerald Isle" ($695 to $745, not including air fare); "Grand Tour of Europe" ($1,238 to $1,448, not including air fare); Iberia ($515 to $695, not including air fare); the Swiss Alps ($549 to $1,069, not including air fare); and Russia ($1,127 to $1,157, not including air fare).

Less expensive bus tours are offered all over Europe by **Cosmos Tourama**, *95-25 Queens Blvd., Rego Park, NY 11374; (212)489-7776.* A tour of the great Central and Eastern European cities is from $475 to $577, not including air fare. A tour of overland Russia through Eastern Europe and Scandinavia is $733, not including air fare. Southern Spain and Portugal is $583, not including air fare.

Study tours

American Leadership Study Groups (ALSG), *Airport Drive, Worcester, MA 01602,* sponsors scores of educational tours throughout Europe. The "Classical Adventure" tour, for example, visits Athens, Delphi, Brindisi, Sorrento, Pompeii, Capri, Rome, and Florence with guides who explain the history behind the sights. The price from New York varies from $1,299 to $1,399. The "Europe East and West" tour visits London, Paris, West and East Berlin, Warsaw, Cracow, Auschwitz, Prague, Vienna, Munich, and the Rhineland for $1,989 (also from New York).

Inexpensive, educational tours are operated by the International Student Travel Conference (ISTC), a coalition of student travel bureaus. Contact the **Council on International Educational Exchange,** *205 E. 42nd St., New York, NY 10017; (212)661-1450,* for information.

CRUISING EUROPE

Imagine sipping a strawberry daiquiri while lounging on the sunny deck of a cruise ship en route to the destination of your choice. Sounds a lot better than trying to keep awake while driving there, or trying to stretch your cramped legs on a train or plane!

Cruising can be a wonderful, convenient means of travel, especially for people who love boats and meeting people, who haven't traveled before, or who have trouble getting around on their own. The variety of crusies out there is overwhelming. How do you choose between them? To make it easier for you, we've dug up the goods on some of the best cruises.

In England. Cunard's *QEII* and *Sagafjord* can take you from the East Coast to England for between $1,350 and $3,985. Cunard also has special $699 one-way fares for return flights on the Concorde. **Cunard**, *555 Fifth Ave., New York, NY 10017; (800)528-6273.*

In Greece. Autumn is a good time to cruise the Greek Isles. Cunard's *Vistafjord* makes a 12-day trip to Greece, Israel, Egypt, Malta, and Italy, calling at Rhodes, Alanya, Limassol, Haifa, Alexandria, Valetta, and Capri. The price is $2,140 to $4,560. **Cunard**, *address above.*

Sun Line's *Stella Maris* and *Stella Oceanis* make four- and seven-day Mediterranean cruises, calling at Rhodes, Alexandria, Port Said, Ashod, Samos, Kusadasi, and Piraeus. The cost aboard the *Oceanis* is $1,075 to $2,205; aboard the *Maris* it's $615 to $1,080. **Sun Line Cruises**, *One Rockefeller Plaza, New York, NY 10020; (800)872-6400.*

Epirotiki Line's *Pegasus*, *Jupiter*, and *Atlas* also cruise the Greek Isles. **Epirotiki Line**, *551 Fifth Ave., New York, NY 10076.*

In Scandinavia. Cruises through the land of the Midnight Sun are made by Royal Viking Cruise Line's *Royal Viking Sea*. Two-week cruises of Scandinavia are from $3,676 to $11,000. Cunard and Royal Cruise Line also sail in this northern region. **Royal Viking Cruise Line**, *One Embarcadero Center, San Francisco, CA 94111.*

Society Expeditions cruises the route of the Vikings, visiting Bergen, the Shetland Islands, the Faeroes, the Heimaey and Surtsey Islands, and Reykjavik, Greenland. The 16-day trip starts at $3,990, including air fare. **Society Expeditions**, *723 Broadway E., Seattle, WA 98102; (206)285-9400.*

In Germany. The KD German Rhine line offers romantic river cruises that sail down the Rhine and Moselle rivers. KD's four-country Rhine cruises visit Holland, Germany, France, and Switzerland in five days. These cruises start at $840. Three-day Moselle River cruises between Koblenz and Trier start at $320. **Rhine Cruise Agency**, *Dietrich Neuhold Corp., 170 Hamilton Ave., White Plains, NY 10601; (914)948-3600.*

Sizing up a cruise

The average cruise costs about $200 a day per person. A typical one-week cruise is $1,000 to $2,000 per person. On the surface, that seems a lot of money. But when you consider that accommodation, food, entertainment, and often even air fare are included, it's not so bad.

Nonetheless, when you're paying that kind of money, you should make sure you're getting a good deal. Before you sign up, consider the following questions:

• What is and isn't included in the price? Does it cover air fare? Food, sports, and recreation should be included.

• How much will you have to pay in tips? You can expect to tip room stewards and waiters $2 to $3 each per day. The busboy and wine steward will expect $1 to $1.50 a day. Bartenders and hairdressers are tipped also. This can add up to as much as $200 during the course of the trip!

• What types of staterooms are available, and what do they cost? Large, upper-deck rooms with windows are the most expensive. Small, inside rooms without windows are the cheapest.

• How much does it cost to travel alone? Prices are based on double occupancy, so you will pay a supplement of 10% to 75% if you want a room to yourself. Most lines can provide a roommate if you prefer.

• Is it cheaper if more than two share a room? The answer should be yes. Many lines offer discounts to third and fourth persons in a cabin. And discounts also are usually available for children.

• Are there discounts on travel between your home city and the departure point? Most lines offer air/sea deals. Sometimes air transportation is free. Some lines offer a cruise-only option for passengers who prefer to make their own way to the departure port.

• Are cruises less expensive during the off-season? Yes. Cruises are several-hundred dollars less during the off-season. In Europe, the lowest fares are during the winter.

• Can you save money by booking in advance? Yes. But you also can get a reduction in price if you book at the last minute.

• What are the penalties for cancellations? If you cancel after the deadline for final payment, you probably will be unable to get a full refund. Some lines offer cancellation insurance.

• For more information, write for a free copy of Cruise Line International Association's booklet *Answers to the Most Asked Questions About Cruising, 17 Battery Place, Suite 631, New York, NY 10004.*

Discounts on cruises

A number of discount cruise clubs and agencies offer inexpensive rates on expensive cruise lines. Some of these organizations are listed below:

• **The Cruise Line**, *(800)327-3021*, offers savings up to 50% on advance and last-minute bookings. No membership fees are charged.

• **Grand Circle Travel**, *(800)221-2610*, offers cruises up to 40% off for last-minute bookings. It also offers tours for travelers over 50.

• **Last Minute Cruise Club**, *(213)519-1717*, offers 50% discounts on cruises.

• **Spur of the Moment Cruises Inc.**, *(800)343-1991*, offers half-price cruises to last-minute passengers.

One last tip

Before signing on for a cruise, find out what sorts of passengers will be on board (will they be college students, singles, elderly people, families?), and what sorts of activities are planned. Once you are on board, you are stuck there!

TRAIN TRIPS

Trains can be a romantic and comfortable way to travel the world. Or they can be cramped and torturous. We have ferreted out some of the world's most inviting and exotic train trips for those of you who would like to plan round-the-world voyages.

You can spoil yourself during a luxurious (but short) four-hour train trip aboard the Nouvelle Premiere from Strasbourg to Paris. Passengers are served the same haute cuisine as at Joël Rebouchon's three-star Paris restaurant, Jamin. One-way fare is $67; meals start at about $45. **French National Railroads**, *610 Fifth Ave., New York, NY 10020; (212)582-2110.*

The Venice Simplon-Orient Express does the famous run between London and Venice. Bordeaux, Paris, Zurich, and Innsbruck are some of the stops it makes on its overnight journey. Pure luxury, from the marquetry and burled wood to the Lalique lamp fixtures. The price of a little more than £570 (about $850) a ticket includes gourmet meals. **Venice Simplon-Orient Express**, *Sea Containers House, 20 Upper Ground, London SE1; tel. (44-1)928-6000.*

The recently inaugurated Al Andalus Express is Spain's luxury train. Lounge cars are decorated in Roaring '20s fashion, and there's entertainment on board. A four-day circle that begins and ends in Seville costs about $879. A 10-day package including air fare from New York is available for $2,122. **Marsans International**, *205 E. 42nd St., New York, NY 10017; (212)661-6565.*

Another new luxury train with restored Edwardian and Victorian cars is the Royal Scotsman, which crosses Scotland on a six-day itinerary. Edinburgh, Inverness, Aberdeen, Kyle, and Mellaig are among the stops. The Royal Scotsman has the oldest dining car in use in the world—it was built in 1891. The cost is about $3,480, including all meals and drinks. The trips are booked by **Abercrombie and Kent International**, *Suite 111, 1420 Kensington Road, Oak Brook, IL 60521; (312)954-2944* or *(800)323-7308.*

Chapter 2

Travel Tips

DOCUMENTS

Passports

All U.S. citizens traveling abroad, including children, must have a valid passport. And yet, most people put off the process of obtaining a passport until the last possible moment. By following certain guidelines, you can save yourself time and money.

Don't delay. Apply for your passport as soon as possible. Apply during low season, July through December; passport agency lines will be shorter. Apply at least four months before your present passport expires. Some countries will not let you enter unless your passport will be valid for another three months after your projected departure date from that country.

Most people delay because they don't want to stand in a line at the passport office, but you can eliminate the physical wait by calling your local post office or district court to find out if it accepts passport applications. Most federal, state, and probate courts and some post offices do accept passport applications. It takes four to eight weeks to obtain a passport through a local center—a little longer than if you went to a passport agency.

First-time applicants

Parents of children under 13 can apply for their children's passports through the mail. But individuals 12 years and older who have never applied for a passport must apply in person at either a passport agency or a participating local center.

In both cases, individuals must produce proof of U.S. citizenship, a completed DSP-11 passport application form, proof of identification, and two passport-size photographs.

The best proof of U.S. citizenship is a certified birth certificate. If this is not available, applicants can submit a certified hospital record, insurance files, or other documentation that includes their name, the date and place of birth, and the proper official signature.

You can obtain a DSP-11 passport application at a local passport center or through the mail from a passport agency. Proof of identity can be a driver's license or an age of majority card. Passport photographs must be two inches by two inches, with your face between 1 and 1 3/8 inches high. The passport fee for a first-time applicant is $42.

Renewals

Renewing applicants who have been issued a passport within the last 12 years and whose most recent passport was issued when they were 16 years old or older, can reapply by mail. The renewal form, DSP-82, must be accompanied by the most recent passport, two identical recent photographs, and a check or money order for $35.

If you are abroad when your passport expires, you can get it renewed at the U.S. Embassy. If you are a woman whose marital status has recently changed, go to the passport office and have your passport amended. If you don't, you may be subject to a fee for keeping the previously issued passport.

Emergency situations

It takes only 10 days for an application to be processed, but sometimes emergencies arise and you need a passport sooner. A letter stating the nature of the emergency should be sufficient proof for the passport agency to grant you a passport more quickly.

Second passports

An American passport can cause you trouble in some regions of the world. But there are ways to get around that if you meet certain requirements. Children, and sometimes grandchildren, of immigrants can obtain passports from the country of their parent's birth. In many countries, once you obtain a passport, you also acquire dual citizenship.

This isn't as easy as it sounds. You must be careful not to unintentionally renounce your U.S. citizenship. The U.S. State Department recommends the following precautions:

- Do not accept a government job from an adopted government.
- Do not serve in another country's military.
- Do not suggest, to friends or anyone else, that you intend to renounce your American citizenship.
- Write a statement of intent to retain U.S. citizenship and send it to a U.S. embassy or consulate.
- File U.S. income tax forms.
- Vote in U.S. elections.
- Use your U.S. passport.

Passport scams

In the classifieds, you'll see advertisements for private passport companies. Some of these ads are legitimate; others are not. Check the advertisement carefully. Does it list a telephone number? Does it have a full address, not just a post office box somewhere in Malaysia? Does it list some ridiculously low or exorbitantly high amount of money? Does it ask for the money right away?

If the advertisement doesn't list a telephone number and doesn't have a legitimate-looking address, chances are the company is a hoax. If you must hand over the money right away, forget it. You'll never see your money again, especially if the sum the company is asking for is less than the cost of obtaining a passport from a passport agency ($35 or $42). Valid companies usually charge you twice as much as a passport agency for their services.

Call the company and ask for more information. If you're turned down, drop the the whole proposition. A legitimate company would be happy to send you more information.

It is best to completely ignore these ads. But if you must have your passport within a week or less, there are companies that can help you obtain a passport quickly and easily.

Passport Plus, a New York-based firm that has been in business for the last five years, is a sound passport company. It offers one-day to one-week processing of passports, visas, and other travel documents. The company's passport fees start at $35, plus a $35 processing fee. Call the toll-free number and request an information package outlining the company's services and prices. **Passport Plus,** *677 Fifth Ave., New York, NY 10022; (800)367-1818.*

U.S. Passport Agencies

Boston Passport Agency
John F. Kennedy Bldg.
Government Center
Boston, MA 02203
(617)565-3930

Chicago Passport Agency
Kluczynski Federal Bldg.
230 S. Dearborn St.
Chicago, IL 60604
(312)353-7155

Honolulu Passport Agency
New Federal Bldg.
300 Ala Moana Blvd.
P.O. Box 50185
Honolulu, HI 96850
(808)041-1920

Houston Passport Agency
1 Allen Center
500 Dallas St.
Houston, TX 77002
(713)229-3600

Los Angeles Passport Agency
Federal Building
11000 Wilshire Blvd.
Los Angeles, CA 90024
(213)209-7075

Miami Passport Agency
Federal Office Bldg.
51 S.W. First Ave.
Miami, FL 33130
(305)536-4681

New Orleans Passport Agency
12005 Postal Services Bldg.
701 Loyola Ave.
New Orleans, LA 70113
(504)589-6161

New York Passport Agency
Rockefeller Center
630 Fifth Ave.
New York, NY 10111
(212)541-7710

Philadelphia Passport Agency
Federal Bldg.
600 Arch St.
Philadelphia, PA 19106
(215)597-7480

San Francisco Passport Agency
525 Market St.
San Francisco, CA 94105
(415)974-9941

Seattle Passport Agency
Federal Building
915 Second Ave.
Seattle, WA 98174
(206)442-7945

Stamford Passport Agency
1 Landmark Square
Stamford, CT 06901
(203)325-3538

Washington Passport Agency
1425 K St. N.W.
Washington, D.C. 20524
(202)523-1355

Visas

Many countries require visas as well as passports. Check with the embassy or consulate of the country you plan to visit. It can tell you how to obtain a visa and what documents are required for processing. You also can obtain this information from a government leaflet entitled *Visa Requirements of Foreign Governments* (M-264), available at U.S. passport agencies. Obtaining a visa takes two to six weeks. Visa fees vary.

Country	Visa Requirements	Additional Information
Andorra	No Visa	
Belgium	No Visa	Visa required for stays longer than 90 days
Britain	No Visa	
Czechoslovakia	Visa Required ($14)	Application, passport, two photos
Denmark	No Visa	Visa required for stays longer than 90 days

Country	Visa Requirements	Additional Information
Finland	No Visa	
France	Visa Required ($9) (one-year visa available for $15)	Application, photo, passport
Greece	No Visa	
Hungary	Visa Required ($10)	Application, passport, two photos
Iceland	No Visa	Visa required for stays longer than 90 days
Ireland	No Visa	Visa required for stays longer than 90 days
Italy	No Visa	Visa required for stays longer than 90 days
Liechtenstein	No Visa	
Luxembourg	No Visa	
Monaco	Visa Required	Same requirements as France
Netherlands	No Visa	
Norway	No Visa	
Poland	Visa Required ($18)	Application, two photos, passport
Portugal	No Visa	
Romania	Visa Required	
Spain	No Visa	Visa required for stays longer than six months
Sweden	No Visa	Visa required for stays longer than 90 days
Switzerland	No Visa	Visa required for stays longer than 90 days
U.S.S.R.	Visa Required	Visa obtained through travel agents only
West Germany	No Visa	Visa required for stays longer than 90 days

Travel Scams

A woman (I'll call her Grace) saw an irresistible ad in the local newspaper. A travel company was offering three-night packages to Acapulco or Cancun for $149.

When she called the toll-free number about the offer, Grace was told this was a special deal to initiate people into a home-shopping club, where members could buy major appliances at drastic discounts. Though not interested in refrigerators, microwaves, or washing machines, Grace was tempted to join anyway, just to get the cheap trip.

She asked for details. The club representative told her that she would be flown round trip from her hometown on a scheduled airline and would stay at a first-class, oceanfront hotel. Grace found the hotel listed in a popular travel guide—it was a first-class hotel.

Grace said she wanted to think about it and asked the representative to send her brochures and other information about the trip and the club. The representative answered that the trips were on a limited-availability basis, there were no brochures, and Grace would have to act immediately if she wanted the trip.

Saying she would send a check, Grace asked for the address (none appeared in the ad). The representative told her that the club would not accept mail payments and that a messenger would come to her door that afternoon to pick up the check in person.

Grace didn't go for it. A good thing, because she probably would have lost her money. When she called a couple weeks later to see if the offer was still available, the telephone had been disconnected. Grace was potential prey for one of the most common con games running: travel scams.

The travel-scam industry has become so big it's almost an epidemic. Every day, companies are set up to bilk bargain hunters of their hard-earned money. Con artists have found travel to be the ideal bait for their traps; who wouldn't fall for a luxurious vacation at an incredible price?

It's also very difficult to catch these bogus operations in action. The companies may go into business, take in hordes of money, and close up shop in as little as a month's time. They usually don't reveal addresses and quietly disconnect their phones, often starting over with a new name, a new phone number, and a new list of suckers. It's almost impossible to trace them. Checking them out with local Better Business Bureaus most likely turns up nothing, because the scoundrels come and go before any complaints can be lodged against them.

Tricks of the trade

If you can't catch them in the act, how can you protect yourself? The best way to be safe is to practice preventive shopping. In other words, be aware of the marks of con operations. You will find them outlined below. If you find an offer that has any of these characteristics, stay away from it.

• **You're a winner!** Here, the con artist sends you a postcard or calls you to explain that you've won a fantastic vacation offer. Usually no address is printed on the card, only a phone number. Not all offers solicited this way are fake, but you must be careful.

• **Special of the day.** If you receive a postcard or respond to an advertisement, the telephone representative may tell you that you've called during a special offer and quote you a price that's even less than that stated on the card or ad. This is a sure tip-off that something's not kosher.

• **Vapid vagaries.** Ask for specifics about the trip. Get names of airlines and hotels. If the representative is reluctant to tell you anything or uses generalizations, such as "five-star hotels" and "major airlines," press for more information. If you fail to get it, say no.

• **Nothing in print.** Any reputable travel company will have brochures and information about its offers. If the company's representative tells you he has no brochures or literature, the offer could be bogus.

• **Now or never.** If you ask a telephone salesperson for more information or say you would like to mull the offer over, he may tell you that the offer is good only on that day and will not be repeated. This is a common tactic of swindlers. They want as much money as they can get in as little time as possible.

• **Pay the messenger.** Absolutely never bite at an offer that requires you to hand over a check to a messenger. No reputable travel company needs to do business this way. This, again, is one of the shyster's ways to get your money quickly—without allowing you to find out where he's located.

• **Pay by credit card.** Many scam operators will ask for your credit card number and expiration date over the phone. It's difficult to judge the legitimacy of a company by this procedure alone. After all, many perfectly honest telemarketing businesses require you to give your charge number over the phone. Before you do it, though, be sure you have evidence that the offer actually exists.

If you do get stung on a credit card payment, you may be able to get out of it by complaining to the credit company and getting them to refuse to pay by credit card.

Other hooks and traps

The preceding information pertains mainly to outright scams—those that literally steal your money without giving you anything in return. Other travel offers, while not illegal, are often based on misleading information and usually come with hidden costs and conditions. The following are some widely practiced schemes.

• **The unbelievable air fare.** You've probably seen ads for these in your Sunday newspaper travel sections. The ads tout air fares of $39 round trip to Hawaii, for example. And when you call the number, you find that the $39 fare is true. But you also find out that, to get the fare, you must purchase a hotel package that may cost $800 to $1,000 or more. Often the ads neglect to tell you that part! If you find an offer like this, shop around. You'll probably find a complete air/hotel package, without the phenomenal advertised fare, for less.

• **The two-for-one...plus.** These offers generally provide hotel accommodations for two and air fare for one. You must book the additional air fares through the companies offering the deals. The air fares they come up with are usually hundreds of dollars more than the fares you could book elsewhere.

• **The time-share arm twister.** Many basement-priced travel packages are sold to induce travelers to buy time-share properties. These may be legitimate bargains, but the vacations tend to be anything but fun. If you book trips of this type, you'll probably spend your vacation being shuttled around to look at properties, subjected to relentless hard-sell pressure, and treated rudely if you don't want to buy. According to the American Society of Travel Agents, you can smell a time-share trap if the offer requires you to earn a minimum salary. Travel companies solely in business to sell travel have no need and no business asking for this information.

The coupon wars

Beware of coupon brokers. If you buy a ticket from one, you may not be allowed to get on the plane.

Airlines have begun confiscating tickets issued by coupon brokers and leaving the ticket buyers stranded at boarding gates all over the world. According to a recent *Wall Street Journal (WSJ)* report, airlines are cracking down on the coupon brokers' practice of selling frequent-flier coupons to the public. The airlines fear that the coupon brokers are taking away too much business; travelers would, of course, rather buy their tickets at the lower prices offered by coupon brokers than pay the full fares offered by the airlines.

How exactly do coupon brokers work? They purchase awards from travelers who are members of airlines' frequent-flier programs. Then they sell these awards, or coupons, to the public. The coupon brokers reissue the coupons in the names of the purchasers, who can redeem them for tickets with their travel agents. Generally, brokers sell the coupons for 10% to 50% less than the airline's ticket prices, depending on the length of the trip (how many miles the coupon is worth) and the class of service. You usually reap the most savings on first- and business-class.

It is not illegal for coupon brokers to do their business. It is, however, against the airlines' rules, which prohibit the sale of frequent-flier awards. Until recently, airlines looked the other way regarding the sale of coupons by their recipients, not wanting to lose the business of their frequent-flying customers. But now, they're fighting back.

According to the *WSJ* report, TWA, United Airlines, and American Airlines have settled out of court a case against one of the largest brokers in the United States. In the settlement, the broker agreed not to buy or sell frequent-flier coupons of those three airlines. (Caution: Don't buy coupons of these airlines from any broker.) And TWA also filed a suit against another broker, accusing the company of fraud for selling nontransferable coupons to unknowing buyers.

Most airlines with frequent-flier programs also have set up new rules making it far more difficult to use coupons bought from brokers. Now, in an effort to catch brokered coupons, many airlines require passengers to redeem their coupons for tickets directly with the airlines, not with travel agents. And many airlines have blacklisted travel agencies that are affiliated with coupon brokers (*WSJ* lists Premier Travel as one such agency). So if you buy a ticket through a blacklisted agency, even if no coupon is involved, you may risk having the ticket confiscated by the airline. Then you lose the money you spent on that ticket, unless the coupon broker agrees to give you a refund (brokers are under no obligation to do this). On top of that, you also have to shell out the fare for a new ticket to get you where you're going.

The current war between airlines and coupon brokers may one day put the brokers out of business. At present, coupon brokers are a very economical way to go, but the risks are considerable and growing every day. If you're looking for bargain air fares, be wary of coupon brokers. If you can't resist dealing with them, follow the guidelines listed below. By doing so, you will at least minimize your risks and may avoid having your tickets snatched at the boarding gate.

Tips for dealing with coupon brokers
• Use coupons for first- and business-class travel.
• Never buy a coupon unless the broker will reissue it in your name.

• Remember that it usually takes five or six weeks to receive the coupon in your name.

• Many coupons have blackout dates (when the coupon is invalid) during holidays or peak traveling periods. Make sure you know about these dates before buying the coupon. If the broker cannot tell you, check with the airline.

• Coupons have expiration dates. Make sure the broker tells you when the coupon expires before you buy.

• Check with the broker about getting a refund should the airline not accept your ticket. If the broker does not offer refunds, shop elsewhere.

• And, of course, if you buy a coupon from a broker, never mention this fact to airline personnel.

AIRLINE INFORMATION

Airplane seating

Infrequent flyers do not necessarily know how to select the best seat for personal comfort. Contact the airline ahead of time and ask for a seating chart. The larger airlines will usually be glad to accommodate you. From the seating chart, you can find out how much leg room a seat has, how wide it is, and if it is located near the galley, bathrooms, or movie area.

If the airline does not keep or refuses to send you a seating chart, let the following tips guide you to the right seat:

• If you want to sleep, ask for a seat away from the partitions, toilets, galleys, or movie areas.

• To avoid sitting with young children, choose a seat far away from the front row where children are customarily placed (although front row seats are in the nonsmoking section and do allow for early disembarkation).

• If you're traveling alone, come aboard right before take-off. The stewardesses will usually let you sit in any of the free seats.

• Aisle seats are safer in the event of a necessary evacuation. Make sure you have access to both exits.

High in the sky

All drinks free	Charge for champagne	Free wine only	No drinks free
Air France	Austrian	Air Portugal	Aer Lingus
Air Lanka	Olympic	Air Zimbabwe	Air Canada
lAir New Zealand	Swissair		Air India
Austrian Airlines	UTA		Alitalia
Cathay Pacific			American Airlines
Dan Air			Ansett
El Al			British Airways
Faucett Peruvian			British Caledonian
Gulf Air			Brymon Airways
Japan Airlines			BWIA
Philippine Airlines			Caribbean
Qantas			Continental
SAA			CP Air
SIA			Delta
Varig			Eastern
			Finnair
			Iberia
			Northwest
			Pan Am
			Sabena
			SAS Scandinavian
			TWA
			United
			Virgin Atlantic

Airline drinking

Time was, those with a predilection for spirits in the sky had to fly first- or business-class for free drinks. Those in economy-class were forced to shell out a bundle for a buzz—$2 to $3 or more for watered-down rotgut Scotch on the rocks.

Today, however, more and more airlines are offering free drinks to their economy-class passengers. You can order anything you want on some; on others, some drinks are free, some are not.

Carry-on luggage

Baggage is a nuisance. You worry about it being lost or

damaged. And you hate to stand around waiting for it after the flight. But some travelers can avoid this frustrating procedure. If you're going to Europe for a few days, you can pack the essentials in a carry-on bag. Whatever you don't pack, you can buy.

Carry-on luggage can be stored under the seat or in the overhead bin. If you want to store it under you seat, choose an aisle seat. Due to the plane's shape, space under window seats varies. Buy small, flexible luggage. Rigid leather luggage will not bend easily into a top space. And try to fit everything you need into one bag. Domestic airlines are especially strict about the amount of carry-on luggage allowed.

Overhead bins, which are larger and more uniform in size, are a better place to store luggage than under yolur seat. In the past few years, most airlines have expanded their overhead bin space. Most of the newer planes have bins that can hold up to 180 pounds. Just remember that it is inconsiderate to take an entire bin for yourself.

TERRORISM

Terrorism in the air

Terrorists tend to see the United States as the imperialist giant of the modern world. Because of this, hijackings, though rare, are more possible on an American carrier than on any other. Fortunately, there are ways to protect yourself:

• Get a boarding pass before you arrive at the airport. The faster you get through security checks to the more protected waiting area, the better.

• Take a charter flight when possible. Charters are of little political interest to terrorists. And because bookings aren't always firm, these flights are too much trouble for hijackers.

• If you can't take a charter, take a direct flight. The fewer times you stop for new passengers, the less the chance of picking up hijackers. Take precautions to avoid planes that stop at locations where disturbances have occurred.

• Avoid target airlines. When flying to Europe, consider European

lines, such as Swissair, KLM, and SAS. A recent *Newsweek* report
suggests you try Eastern bloc airlines. However, while security on
communist airlines is generally tighter, Eastern bloc airlines, as a
regional group, have the worst record in the world for accidents.
Their chances of crashing are 10 times worse than the worldwide
average.
• Stay alert. Keep an eye out for suspicious people or objects.
Check under your seat when you board your plane. Inform airline
personnel if you notice an abandoned suitcase.
• Keep a low profile. Don't advertise your American identity.
Leave the expensive jewelry, clothes, luggage at home. Don't
hang out at known American gathering spots.
• If your plane is hijacked, stay calm. Do not make any sudden
moves. Ask for permission before getting up, even if it's to go to
the bathroom. Do not argue with a hijacker, no matter how
ridiculous his argument. If you are chastised for doing something
(reading a magazine for example), quickly comply. No matter
what happens, remember that the hijacker holds the cards (and
gun).

Terrorism on land

Terrorist incidents against Americans and their allies are much
more common on land than in the air. The best defense against
terrorism is to be inconspicuous. Do not make it obvious that you
are an American. Do not travel around in a limousine or cavort
with controversial public figures. Be especially careful if you are
a wealthy white male who is either working for the military or is a
symbol of power (the president of a major corporation, for example). To find out if you're traveling into a high-risk area
contact the **Citizen's Emergency Center,** *(202)632-5225.*

HEALTH AND SAFETY

Safe flights

Although these tips may seem obvious to the seasoned
traveler, they may save your life in an emergency:
• Listen to the flight attendants' preflight talk.

You should also read the safety card on the back of the seat in front of you.

• Keep you seat belt fastened whenever you are in your seat. You may see many people unfasten theirs, but it is definitely safer to keep it on. Air turbulence is the leading cause of passenger injury. And air turbulence can come out of nowhere; don't be fooled by beautiful, seemingly calm, blue skies.

• Make sure you know where the exits are. Notice any obstacles that could prevent you from reaching them in an emergency.

• No seat is injury-proof. The best seat is probably an aisle seat near an emergency exit.

• If a crash occurs, follow the evacuation instructions of the crew. If the crew does not immediately respond to the emergency, it is probably incapacitated. You'll have to move on your own. Check for flames before opening the emergency exit. If there are flames, you will have to find another escape route.

• Smoke inhalation is especially dangerous in the enclosed area of an airplane; stay close to the floor until you get out. Once you get out, get as far away from the airplane as possible.

Travelers' insurance and assistance programs

Be prepared. Medical emergencies occur anytime, anywhere. And some American insurance companies do not cover you when you travel abroad. (Medicare and Medigap are two examples.) Before traveling, contact your insurance company to make sure you're covered and to find out what exactly you're covered for. If you're not covered under your present plan, and your company does not offer travelers' insurance riders that you can add to your plan, buy a short-term traveler's insurance policy from another company.

One company that covers medical expenses in foreign countries is **Access America,** *600 Third Ave., New York, NY 10016; (800)851-2800,* a subsidiary of Blue Cross/Blue Shield. It offers a $20,000 family policy for a two-week trip outside the United States for $97 and a $10,000 single policy for $61.

Gold MasterCard holders are eligible for overseas medical insurance through their credit cards. They do not have to pay insurance through their credit cards. They do not have to pay anything extra for the service, but coverage is limited to $2,500 per person. Other benefits include $10,000 transportation coverage if the patient needs to be flown to another hospital for adequate care and a 24-hour, toll-free number to call for the names of English-speaking physicians.

Other insurance companies that offer short-term travelers' insurance policies are Aetna, CNA, Mutual of Omaha, Safeco, and the Exeter Hospital Aid Society.

You can also join a travelers' assistance program to procure medical insurance abroad. These organizations offer a broader spectrum of services, including medical, financial, and legal assistance.

Europ Assistance, *Worldwide Services Inc., 1333 F St. N.W., Suite 300, Washington, DC 20004; (800)821-2828,* is a travelers' assistance organization that offers a special Trip Protection program for worldwide travelers. To become eligible for the program, you pay either a one-year membership fee of $5 or a three-year membership fee of $14. Once you've joined the organization, you can apply for trip coverage. The Trip Protection program costs $30 to $50 per person, depending upon the number of days you will be out of the country. Benefits include $5,000 medical coverage, legal assistance in foreign legal matters, including bail posting, transmission of emergency messages, emergency cash advances if you become stranded due to theft or loss, and special arrangements for your family if you fall ill while traveling and require hospitalization.

NEAR, *1900 N. MacArthur Blvd., Oklahoma City, OK 73127; (405)949-2500,* is another international travelers' assistance organization. Unlike most companies, it covers you when you travel in the United States, as well as outside the United States. NEAR offers family memberships for $180 per year and single memberships for $120 per year. It also offers short-term foreign hospitalization coverage for $3 a day, per person, but you must already be a member. Non-members must pay $4 a day, per person. This short-term coverage includes $100,000 health insurance with a $50 deductible.

Though most travelers' assistance programs charge a membership fee for blanket coverage, some companies offer medical assistance for free, although you still pay doctors' fees.

Intermedic, *777 Third Ave., New York, NY 10017,* publishes a directory of English-speaking physicians worldwide, who charge standard fees for members of Intermedic. Office visits range from $30 to $40, and house calls range from $50 to $60.

The **International Association for Medical Assistance to Travelers** (IAMAT), *417 Center St., Lewiston, NY 14092,* is a nonprofit organization that collects and distributes medical information worldwide for the benefit of travelers. And it doesn't charge a membership fee. When you join, you receive a directory listing English-speaking member doctors in more than 1,400 cities world-wide. These doctors are trained in Western medical practices and meet Western standards. They are on-call 24-hours a day. IAMAT also offers medical services at fixed prices worldwide. Member doctors charge $20 for office visits, $30 for house calls, and $40 for night calls, Sundays, and holidays.

IAMAT membership entitles you to a Travelers' Clinical Record. You can have your physician fill it out and then carry it with you on your journey. You also receive a World Immunization Chart, a Malaria Risk Chart, a World Schistosomiasis Risk Chart, and a World Climate Chart. If you require any other health and safety information, IAMAT will be happy to help you.

Insurance checklist

People have different needs. Make sure your insurance policy covers the areas you care about most. Does your policy include trip cancellation, hijacking provisions, evacuation, baggage loss, emergency medical and/or legal expenses, rental car collision, lost deposits, and travel company bankruptcy? The following is a list of other points that you should keep in mind:

• Credit card companies often offer some form of travelers' benefits. Call your company to find out if you are eligible for any available benefits.

• Individuals with chronic ailments should make sure that their current policy covers their existing problems while they're overseas. If not, they may need additional insurance.

• Some insurance companies do not pay your medical expenses while you are abroad, although they will reimburse you once you return to the United States. You are forced to shoulder the costs of your medical treatments until you get home. To be safe, get a policy that pays outright.

• Senior citizens should be especially careful about insurance. Many companies do not cover medical expenses abroad for senior citizens. Call your company and make sure you're covered. If not, buy a short-term major medical policy.

• Some homeowners' insurance policies cover baggage loss. See if yours does before paying extra to get a baggage-loss rider tacked on to your insurance policy.

Immunizations

Most European countries do not require immunizations or proof of immunizations other than those shots recommended for all U.S. citizens—polio, diphtheria, and tetanus. But there are important exceptions. The following is an immunization chart. If you have questions about a country that is not listed, contact the **International Association for Medical Assistance to Travelers,** *736 Center St., Lewiston, NY 14092.*

Immunization key: C—Cholera; P—Plague; D—Dengue Fever; H—Infectious Hepatitis; R—Rabies; TL—Infectious louse-borne Typhus; T—Typhoid Fever; Y—Yellow Fever; M—Routine Immunizations (Dipththeria, Polio, Tetanus).

1. Vaccination certificate not required, except from travelers who, within the last 14 days, have been in a country any part of which is infected.

2. Vaccination certificate is required of travelers coming from these infected countries:

Angola, Benin, Botswana, Burundi, Cameroon, Central African Republic, Chad, Congo, Equatorial Guinea, Ethiopia, Gabon, Gambia, Ghana, Guinea, Guinea-Bissau, Ivory Coast, Kenya, Liberia, Malawi, Mali, Mauritania, Niger, Nigeria, Rwanda, Sao Tome and Principe, and Senegal.

Country	Immuniza-tion Code	Country	Immuniza-tion Code
Andorra	M4	Madeira Islands	Y1, M4
Austria	M4	Monaco	M4
Belgium	M4	Netherlands	M4
Bulgaria	M4	Norway	M4
Canary Islands	M5	Poland	M4
Cyprus	H3, T3, M4, D9	Portugal	Y1, 2, 8, M4
Czechoslovakia	M4	Romania	M4
Finland	M4	Spain	M4
France	M4	Sweden	M4
E. and W. Germany	M4	Switzerland	M4
Gibraltar	M4	Turkey	H3, R6, T3, M4, D9
Greece	Y1, T3, M4		
Hungary	M4		
Iceland	M4	U.S.S.R.	H3, P5, TL7, T3, M4
Ireland	M4		
Italy	M4		
Liechtenstein	M4	United Kingdom	M4
Luxembourg	M4	Yugoslavia	M4

3. Vaccination is recommended for travelers traveling outside tourist areas, traveling extensively in the interior, and working in the country.

4. Vaccination is recommended for all travelers.

5. Vaccination is recommended only for persons who will be occupationally exposed to rodents. Tourists traveling temporarily in the interior will be sufficiently protected against plague by taking three grams of sulfonamide daily.

6. Pre-exposure rabies vaccines are recommended only for people on working assignments. Children should be told not to pet animals.

7. Risk exists for persons living or working in the interior. Apply insecticide powder to clothes, and practice good personal hygiene. If infested, tetracycline will cure you.

8. Requirement only applies to travelers arriving in or destined for the Azores and Madeira. No certificate is required of transit passengers at Funchal, Porto Santo, and Santa Maria.

9. Risk exists of dengue fever outbreak. This disease is transmitted by the Aedes mosquitoes. If risk is present, apply mosquito repellents such as diethyltoluamide or 2-elhylhexane-diol, 1,3 several times a day. If there are window screens, use bed nets.

For current immunization information, contact **The Georgetown University School of Medicine,** *International Health Service, (202)625-7379.* The office is open Monday through Friday, 8:30 a.m. to 5 p.m. Or call your State Health Department to find out what local clinics can provide immunizations and immunization information.

Malaria

Sixty Anopheles (mosquito) species are malaria-parasite carriers. Each specie is region- and host-specific and has its own feeding pattern. For example, one specie may live in southern Portugal, bite both humans and donkeys, and bite its prey several times in one feeding period. If you're going to an area where malaria is a risk, find out about the mosquitos in the area before you go. Do they eat at sundown? Do they eat after midnight? Do they feed serveral times during a feeding period? Where do they like to feed? Once you reach your destination, follow these special precautions before night sets in:

• Make sure your room has tightly fitting window and door screens without any holes (or sealed windows and central air-conditioning). Cover any holes with adhesive tape.

• If your room doesn't have window screens, you should have bed nets. Bed nets should be white so mosquitos are clearly visible. They should be made of stiff cotton with a tightly woven border and a zipper opening. A netting with 26 holes per inch should provide sufficient protection.

• During the day, bed nets should be left hanging in a knot from the ceiling. At night, before you enter the bed, lower the netting, tuck the ends under the mattress, and check for any mosquitoes caught inside. Also, look for any new holes that require mending.

• Use mosquito repellent on all exposed areas of your body. Reapply it every two to three hours. Use only repellents with the active ingredient DEET (N,N-diethyl-meta-toluamide).

• Cover food and cooking utensils and spray your room several times a day with a pyrethrin insecticide. Spray everything—bed nets, walls, furniture, baseboards, in closets and corners, under the bed and the sink, and even behind pictures and curtains. Do not open the windows while spraying and leave the room immediately after spraying.

• Beginning at dusk, wear only long-sleeved shirts and long pants. Do not wear dark clothing, perfume, or cologne, which attracts mosquitoes.

Malaria suppressants

No drugs prevent malaria infection, but there are drugs that suppress malaria symptoms after the infection has been introduced into the red blood cells. These drugs eliminate the parasites of the fatal form of malaria, P. falciparum, and the benign form P. malariae, but they do not always prevent a delayed first attack or relapse of the benign forms P. vivax or P. ovale, which may appear several years later.

Travelers to malarious regions must take an antimalarial drug at regular intervals. Start taking the drug two weeks before you depart. Continue taking the drug for at least six weeks after you return home. Even if you are just staying in a malarious area overnight or in transit between flights during the dark hours, you should still take the entire cycle of suppressants.

Chloroquine (brand names Aralen, Avloclor, Resochin, and Nivaquine) is the most common antimalarial drug. But chloroquine has several side effects. It is very bitter and causes nausea and diarrhea. It may also cause headaches and blurring of vision. Persons with liver problems, alcoholism, or blood disorders should not take chloroquine; it may harm their livers.

Amodiaquine, brand names Camoquine and Flavoquine, is an alternative to chloroquine. It does not have the bitter taste characteristic of chloroquine, but it is not available in the United States, the United Kingdom, or Canada.

In some malarious regions of the world, P. falciparum has developed a resistance to chloroquine in response to its frequent

Malaria Suppressants

Countries Where Sold	Brand Name	Manufacturer	Generic Name	Salt Content/Tablet	Active Compound	No. of Tablets
Canada and overseas	Aralen	Winthrop	chloroquine diphosphate	250 mg	150 mg	2 weekly
United States	Aralen	Winthrop	chloroquine diphosphate	500 mg	300 mg	1 weekly
Europe and some malarious regions	Resochin	Bayer	chloroquine diphosphate	250 mg	150 mg	2 weekly
France and some malarious regions	Nivaquine	Societe Specia	chloroquine sulfate	410 mg	300 mg	1 weekly
France and Some malarious regions	Flavoquine	Roussel	amodiaquine dihydrochloride	260 mg	200 mg	2 weekly
United States and most malarious regions	Fansidar	Hoffmann-LaRcche	sulfadoxine pyrunetganube	500 mg	25 mg	1 weekly
United Kingdom and some malarious regions	Maloprim	Burroughs Wellcome	dapsone pyrimethamine	100 mg	12.5 mg	1 weekly

use. In these areas, the most commonly used drug is sulfadoxine-pyrimethamine, brand name Fansidar. This drug is available in the United States, but not Canada. (Pregnant women should not take this drug or travel to regions where P. falciparum is resistant to chloroquine. Fansidar can cause birth defects.)

To obtain a World Wide Malaria Risk Chart, contact the **International Association for Medical Assistance to Travelers,** *address above.* This chart will tell you what countries are malarious regions, what species inhabit these regions, and their feeding habits, as well as what countries are malaria-free.

For more health and safety information, contact the **Citizen's Emergency Center,** *(202)632-5225*. It provides country-specific precautions, including any reports of labor unrest, anti-American activity, disease outbreaks, lack of hotel accommodations, etc. The office is open Monday through Friday, 8 a.m. to 5 p.m.

Medical precautions

If you take a few precautions before you go abroad, you will be better prepared for a medical emergency. The following is a list of precautions to take before you leave:

• If you have any chronic illnesses, have your doctor prepare a simple typed medical history for you to carry on your person. If you need medical attention while abroad, this will help a foreign doctor treat you more effectively.

• Get a medical bracelet if you have a serious problem, such as epilepsy, allergic reactions to penicillin, or diabetes.

• Many American prescriptions are not available abroad. Take a sufficient supply of medications with you. Just to be safe, ask your doctor for typed copies of your prescriptions, with the generic name of the drug and the dosage given in the metric system.

• Carry all medication in its original packaging, with prescription labeling, to avoid confiscation and legal hassles with customs officials.

• Carry an extra pair of eyeglasses and a copy of your prescription.

• Get a World Health Organization International Certificate of

Vaccination if you need special immunizations to cross borders.
Your doctor or any hospital can provide one.
• If you're traveling to warm weather climates or you expect to go
on several outdoor excursions, you'll need to take insect repellent.
• Travelers to the Mediterranean should take water-purification
tablets along.
• Aspirin, bandaids, and corn plasters are also good to have along.

Medical records

Carrying your medical records abroad could save your life. If
you are in a serious accident and are unconscious, doctors won't
be able to ask your medical history. If, for example, they don't
know you're allergic to penicillin, they may give it to you, setting
off a new problem.

You don't have to carry your whole life history from nose-
bleeds to pregnancies, but you should carry essential information
on your person or a number where a foreign doctor can quickly
and easily find out the necessary information. Following is a list
of information you should keep on your person:
• A brief description of any current problems (high blood
pressure, anemia, diabetes).
• Past medical problems (heart trouble, peptic ulcers, seizures;
include the date).
• Past surgery (include the date).
• Allergies (drugs, bees, alcohol, fir trees).
• Current medication (dilantin, cafregot, phenobarbital, valium).
• Lifestyle (smoking, drinking, heavy caffeine intake).
• Recent statistics (weight, height, blood pressure, pulse; include
the date).
• Recent test results (cardiogram, electroencephalogram, medica-
tion levels; include the date).
• Broken bones (include the date).
• Blood type.
• Any abnormalities that might be helpful or indicative of a
problem not yet discovered.

Jet lag

Your internal clock runs on a fairly regular schedule. But every time you fly into another time zone, you disrupt your internal rhythms. European time is five to seven hours ahead of American time. This sudden change makes travelers become overwhelmingly tired, groggy, and lightheaded. You may develop headaches, backaches, and nausea or even lose your sense of balance and coordination. The following is a list of precautions to take:

• Before you leave, try to prepare your body for the new time zone. If you're going to London, which is five hours ahead of American time, start going to bed an hour earlier and getting up an hour earlier five days before your departure. By the time you depart, your body will have adjusted.

• In the days before you leave and during your flight, try to cut your caffeine intake. Studies show that caffeine makes bodily adjustment more difficult.

• Although many airlines offer alcoholic beverages for free, avoid alcohol. You don't need the added impact of a hangover. If you do indulge, drink wine. The alcohol content is lower than mixed drinks, reducing the impact on your body.

• Eat lightly during your flight. If you eat too heavily, you may feel nauseous.

• Try to sleep during your flight. This will reduce the exhaustion after your flight.

• Once you land, take a few minutes to stretch. Do not go to your hotel to sleep if it is only 5 p.m. Stay awake as long as possible, try to eat a light meal, and remain active. This will allow your body to adjust more quickly to the new timetable and reduce the effects of jet lag.

Digestive problems

Travel tends to aggravate minor physical problems. Your digestive system is particularly vulnerable. Used to a fairly regular diet of food and water, your system may react adversely when you travel abroad. Mealtimes are different. The food is different. Even the water has a different chemical composition. You may become constipated or develop diarrhea. Here are some tips to help you avoid internal chaos:

• Establish a consistent, cautious eating pattern. Allow your body to adjust by eating familiar foods. Introduce unfamiliar delicacies slowly and in small quantities. Avoid fresh cheese. And do not overeat, no matter what the temptation.

• Avoid coffee. Switch to tea temporarily. In Spain, Portugal, and Italy, you should be especially careful about the water. Do not drink tap water. Don't even use it for brushing your teeth. Do not drink uncarbonated sodas or drinks with ice cubes. And avoid milk products.

• Individuals prone to constipation should drink lots of bottled water even in northern Europe. They should also eat bulk foods everyday and set aside a period of time each day for exercise.

• Mild diarrhea can be treated with the European equivalent of Pepto Bismol. More serious diarrhea, accompanied by cramps and nausea, should be treated by an antibiotic, such as Septra. Eliminate solid foods. Drink clear liquids—weak tea, apple juice, and bottled water several times a day. Add extra sugar and salt to your diet. When you start to feel better, begin eating solids again, but go easy. Eat soft, neutral foods (oatmeal, applesauce, rice, toast).

If, after five days, your diarrhea does not go away, or if you develop bloody excrement, contact a doctor. Also, if your child gets diarrhea, seek medical help immediately. Travelers' diarrhea is much harder on children than on adults.

For more information on digestive disorders and ways to avoid problems while traveling, contact the **American Digestive Disease Society,** *7720 Wisconsin Ave., Bethesda, MD 20814; (301)652-9293.*

Hypothermia and frostbite

You're at St. Moritz. Your body is freezing. Your face and hair are dry. And your lips are painfully chapped. You wanted a wonderful winter vacation, but what you got was pain. You were unprepared for the cold weather.

Hypothermia and frostbite are the main worries in winter, especially in the northern climates, where storms can pop up without any warning.

No matter if you're going out for a few minutes or for hours at a time, you should always dress for the possibilities. Wear several layers of light clothing. Layers trap the heat better than a single heavy garment. Loose layers are better for your circulation and easier to take off if your underlayers get wet from perspiration. Your upper layer should be wind-resistant.

Although cotton long johns are the easiest to find, they also get wet more quickly and retain the wetness much longer than long johns with polyester insulation. Try to find polypropylene long johns. Make most of your layers polyester or wool; they will stay dry much longer and protect you more efficiently.

Safety comes before fashion. Don't worry about mussing your hair; wear a hat, preferably a wool one. You lose the most heat through your head. Wear mittens instead of gloves. Your fingers will keep each other warm. Wear two pairs of socks, one thin and the other thick. If your boots are wet inside and you don't have any others, stay inside!

Frostbite is the biggest danger in cold weather. Your fingers, toes, nose, and ears are particularly vulnerable. If you begin to feel pain in your extremities and they turn red, seek shelter. If you cannot immediately go inside, increase your circulation by moving around (walking faster, wiggling the offending parts, doing jumping jacks). If you begin to turn white, you're in trouble. This is the last danger sign your body will give you before your tissues freeze. Seek shelter immediately. Once inside, warm up slowly; it will be a painful process.

Hypothermia (dangerously low body temperature) is another danger in cold weather. (Cross-country skiers, especially, are prone to hypothermia and should be particularly careful.) If someone in your group begins to exhibit confusion, a lack of coordination, or irritation or says he is overheated, get that person inside. Cover him with a blanket, leaving the fingers and toes outside the blanket. The blood in them is too cold to circulate. Get under the blanket with him. Body heat is particularly helpful.

How to avoid hypothermia

• Check with the weather information center before you leave. Don't go out if bad weather is pending.
• If you're going into unfamiliar territory, don't go alone. Carry plenty of water and high-energy food.
• If you're a smoker, limit your smoking; it impedes your circulation.
• Avoid getting wet.
• Watch the other members of your party for signs of frostbite and hypothermia.

Skin protection

The humidity level lowers during the winter, drying out your skin, hair, and lips. To prevent this, wear lip balm. Wash your hair and face at night only, leaving the natural oils on throughout the day. Shave at night. Put moisturizer on at night all over your body, including the heels of your feet; they crack too.

Skiing enthusiasts should be particularly careful. They should wear a protective sunscreen on the exposed parts of their body, including their lips. This protects them from both ultraviolet rays and the activation of the virus that causes herpes simplex. The sunscreen factor should be at least 15.

Oil baths and hair conditioners are two other ways to insulate your body against the damaging effects of the winter.

Out-thinking thieves

Tourists are often easy marks for thieves, who know they are carrying money. Special precautions will lessen the opportunities of thieves. Here's a list of things you can do:
• Carry most of your money in travelers' checks insured for theft.
• Never leave your belongings unattended in airports, hotels, or restaurants.
• Taxi drivers can also rip you off. If a taxi driver doesn't turn his meter on, ask him to turn it on or go get yourself another cab. Otherwise, he may take you to your destination, charge you a high fee, and pocket it himself. If he tries to rip you off, get his cab number and report him.

• If you agree to let someone carry your luggage and load it into a taxi, watch him closely. He could run off with your bag or pretend to load your bags into the taxi while holding some back. You may not realize you've been had until you reach the hotel.

• When registering in hotels, do not put your briefcase on the floor. That makes it a perfect target for a quick grab.

• Keep your valuables in the hotel safe.

• When you go out, always lock your windows and doors, especially those leading to balconies.

• When eating in the hotel restaurant or lounge, never leave your hotel key on the table. A thief can note the room number, go to your room, and rob you when he knows you're out.

• If you're in town for a convention and required to wear a name tag, remove your name tag when you're not in a meeting. Otherwise, thieves will notice your name, find out your room number from the desk clerk, and rob your room while you're out.

• Never let a stranger into the hotel room even if he claims to be on the hotel staff. Call the desk to make sure the person is legitimate before opening the door.

• In crowds walk against the flow of traffic, even if you do get dirty looks. That makes a pickpocket's job much harder.

• If someone jostles you in a crowd, turn around immediately while checking for your wallet. Pickpockets move fast.

• Don't keep your passport and cash in the same place.

• If you carry a purse, carry your cash in your pocket. Cash should be kept in front pants or skirt pockets; pickpockets go for purses and back pockets first. (Money belts are even better. If they are well-attached, they are difficult to pick.)

• Try to get shadowed baggage tags so a thief can't memorize your name and address.

• When shopping do not put your packages down on the ground to get your money out. Put them in front of you where you can see them or keep them in an over-the-shoulder bag. Keep your bag toward the front of your body while walking; if it's too far behind you, someone can reach in and take something out without you knowing until it's too late.

• Sleazy clubs, topless bars, and strip joints are notorious for

scams. Foreigners are easy prey. For example, if you buy a bottle of champagne for a "lady," the bartender, after she's had a few drinks, may come up and exchange the bottle for a half-empty one. By the end of the night, you are charged an exorbitant price for six bottles, while you probably only drank one full bottle of champagne.
• If you lose your checkbook and it is returned, make sure that none of the checks are missing.

Women

Unfortunately, women need to take special precautions when traveling abroad, especially when traveling alone. Attitudes toward women vary from country to country, but here are a few general precautions that women should take when traveling:
• If you're traveling solo, use public transportation whenever possible. The incidences of rape and robbery of lone women in cabs are alarmingly high. As an American, you are an even greater temptation.
• Do most of your traveling in the daytime. If you must go out at night, travel with an acquaintance, especially in southern Europe, where the men tend to be sexually aggressive toward women. There are some locales where you should not go out alone at night, period!
• The less you carry around with you, the easier it will be to run if necessary. Do not overburden yourself with packages or luggage.
• Tell an acquaintance or a desk clerk every time you go out and mention the approximate time of your return. If you don't return, he can alert the local authorities
• Do not wear expensive jewelry or clothes, especially when you're alone. You're inviting trouble.
• In some countries it is difficult for businesswomen to make the proper business contacts. The International Trade Commission in the Department of Commerce should be able to help. It also can advise you about local business customs and markets.
• Men in Italy and Spain like to pinch. Stand with your back against the wall in elevators, and if you're traveling with a friend, ask him to walk behind you in crowds. If you figure out who's

pinching you, turn around and say "Enough." That will usually put an end to it.

• The better class hotels now have special rooms and suites for lone women. These rooms often have lighted mirrors, skirt hangers, hair dryers, and softer decorations. They also tend to be more secure. **Preferred Hotels Worldwide,** *(800)323-7500,* is one such chain. It has hotels in England, Austria, France, Germany, Italy, Norway, and Switzerland.

• Exude self-confidence. This will get you exactly what you ask for.

• Ask the management if the hotel has a floor with extra-security. Ask for a room on that floor.

• If the hotel does not have an extra security floor, ask for a room near an elevator or the public rooms on an upper floor.

• If the desk clerk announces your room number aloud in the lobby, quietly ask for another room.

• Have your key ready before you reach your room, so you don't have to look down and fumble around. Someone could sneak up behind you.

American Express publishes two helpful brochures: "The Business Woman's Travel Guide" and "Have a Safe Trip." Two other publications that are helpful are *The Women's Guide to Business Travel* (Penelope Naylor, Hearst Books, 1981) and *In Another Dimension: A Guide for Women Who Live Overseas* (Nancy J. Piet-Pelon and Barbara Hornby, Intercultural Press, 1985).

ETIQUETTE

European etiquette is more rigid than American etiquette. Certain customs that are perfectly acceptable at home are considered terribly rude in Europe. Some of these differences are obvious; others are not so obvious. For example, cutting your potatoes with a knife is considered an insult to a West German hostess. Knowing the proper etiquette ahead of time could save you and your European host unnecessary trouble.

Standard rules of European etiquette

• Shake hands when introduced and when leaving.
• Never use first names with acquaintances or business associates, unless your foreign acquaintances do.
• Do not put your hands in your pockets when speaking to someone.
• In West Germany, France, Austria, and Switzerland, say "hello" and "good-bye" to shopkeepers and salespersons.
• Avoid political, social, and religious topics in conversation.
• Always wear suits to business engagements, unless told otherwise.
• Unless otherwise stated, men should wear suits to the theater and women should wear cocktail dresses.
• Always make arrangements ahead of time before visiting a private home.
• Flowers are the usual dinner gift. Send an uneven number of cut flowers ahead of your arrival. (Note that some flowers, such as carnations, have a special significance and should be avoided).
• If you make a phone call while staying at a private home, find out the cost of the call and repay your host.
• Wish everyone a "good appetite" before beginning to eat.
• Europeans eat with the fork in their left hands and the knife in their right hands.
• Do not put your hands in your lap. Keep your forearms, not your elbows, on the table.
• Never leave any food on your plate; it is an insult to your hostess.
• Do not give a business gift at the first meeting.
• Never photograph soldiers or military equipment and installations in communist countries.

Austria

Greetings
• An Austrian man often kisses a woman's hand when being introduced. Lay your hand limply in his, and allow him to raise it to his lips.

• A man should wait for a woman to extend her hand before extending his.
• Use occupational titles with the last name when speaking to a male professional.
• Use "Frau" followed by the occupational title when addressing a female professional.
• All women over 20, whether married or not, are addressed as "Frau."

Conversation

• Most professionals address each other by their last names throughout their association.
• Avoid talking about money, religion, divorce, or separation.
• Never call an Austrian a German.
• Do not offer casual compliments. Austrians find this very embarrassing.
• Do not make casual promises. Austrians take promises very seriously.

Public manners

• Men should stand when a woman enters the room and when speaking to a woman who is standing.
• To attract someone's attention, hold up your hand with the index finger extended.
• You must check your coat at public functions.

Dress

• Do not wear shorts in towns or cities, even for casual wear. Men should wear pants and shirts. Women may wear pants, jeans, skirts, or dresses.
• Men should wear suits to dinner parties, women dresses.
• When attending the opera, the theater, or a concert, dress formally.

Table manners

• Serve yourself if food is passed around the table.
• Don't start eating until your hostess begins.
• Don't cut fish or potatoes with a knife. You are implying that

they are undercooked.
• Don't spit seeds into an open palm. Spit them into a closed hand before placing them on the edge of your plate.
• Always break your rolls before biting into them.
• After eating, place your utensils side by side on your plate.

Private homes
• The traditional visiting hour is 3 p.m.
• Never ask to use the bathroom; ask for the W.C. (water closet).
• If staying in a private home, offer to help with the cleaning and pay for any phone calls you make.

Gifts
• When invited to someone's home for a meal, bring flowers or wine. Unwrap the flowers before giving them to your hostess. Don't give red roses or red carnations; the roses are only for lovers and the carnations signify mourning.
• If you're staying with an Austrian family, bring gifts from the United States.
• Business gifts should be useful or interesting, such as a calculator or a fine bottle of bourbon.

Extras
• In restaurants, call the waiter "Herr Ober." Call the waitress "Fraulein."
• Don't expect the waiter to present you with a bill. When finished, tell the waiter what you ate and he will add it up then.
• At hotels, if you want a room with a bath and a toilet, ask for a bath and W.C.
• Don't hail a taxi yourself. Go to a taxi stand or ask the desk clerk at your hotel to call you one.

Belgium and Luxembourg

Greetings
• When introduced, shake hands and repeat your name.
• When you arrive at or leave a business meeting, shake hands with everyone present, including the secretaries.

Conversation

• Always use "Mr.," Mrs.," or "Miss" in front of someone's name.
• Avoid taking sides in political issues or discussing religious or language differences in Belgium.
• If you don't speak Dutch, use English in Flemish Belgium instead of French.
• Learn the Flemish and French names for Belgian cities and use the appropriate name in the proper company.

Public manners

• On public transportation men should allow women to board first, and should not sit until the women are seated.
• Loudness and overexuberance are considered rude.

Dress

• For business meetings, men should wear suits and well-polished shoes. Women should wear dresses or skirts and blouses.
• Dinner guests are expected to wear suits or dresses.
• Engagements that call for formal wear require men to wear tuxedos and women gowns.
• On Sundays in Belgium, everyone dresses in their Sunday best and promenades about town.

Table manners

• If your host offers you a drink before dinner, select a drink from the brands that he lists.
• Husbands and wives are never seated together.
• Formal meals include a fish course requiring special silverware. The fish fork will be on the left side of the plate and will look like a salad fork. The fish knife will be on the right side of the plate and will look like a butter knife.
• The spoon above your plate is for dessert.
• When finished, place your fork and knife horizontally across the top of the plate with the tines of the fork and the point of the knife pointing left.
• After a formal dinner, stay until the cigars have been finished.

Private homes

• Don't call on people before 10 a.m. or after 10 p.m.

Gifts

• If you're invited to dinner in a private home, bring flowers or chocolates. Avoid chrysanthemums. Always bring extra gifts if there are children.

• If you're staying in a private home, bring something American.

• Business gifts are appreciated but not expected. Give a book related to the business or a pen set.

Extras

• In restaurants, never order tea or coffee with a meal. If you wish to order scotch whiskey, ask for "whiskey" because Scotch is a brand of beer.

• Never leave your hotel without leaving your key at the desk.

• Never try to arrange a business meeting for a Saturday.

• American businesswomen who want to entertain a Belgian businessman should make arrangements to pay beforehand. A Belgian businessman will never let a woman pay under any other circumstances.

Bulgaria

Greetings

• Address both men and women as "Comrade" followed by their last names, unless he or she is a doctor, professor, architect, engineer, or priest. In these cases, use the person's professional title.

Conversation

• Avoid political topics and steer wide of social or political conditions in Bulgaria.

• Yes and No gestures are the opposite of those in the United States.

Public manners

• Carry toilet paper and do not be shocked at the bathroom facilities, which are sometimes primitive.

Dress

• Only children wear shorts in the city.

• For casual wear, men should wear shirts and pants, and women should wear skirts, dresses, or pants.

• When invited to dinner in a private home, men should wear suits in the winter and dress pants and a shirt in the summer. Women should wear dresses or skirts.

• Formal wear consists of dark conservative suits and short cocktail dresses.

Table manners

• Use the spoon above the plate for coffee.

• If you don't drink wine, ask for mineral water.

• A hearty appetite is appreciated and expected.

• Conversation is minimal.

• Coffee is always served black.

• Bulgarians are very hospitable, but try to leave by 11 p.m.

Private homes

• Don't ask for an iced drink. Most homes do not have refrigerators.

• If you're staying in a private home, give your passport to the family to register you with the local police; they will get in trouble if they do not do so immediately upon your arrival.

• Ask before taking a bath; the water supply is not dependable.

• Guests are not allowed to help clean.

Gifts

• If you're invited to a meal, bring flowers, candy, or wine. Avoid gladioli and calla lilies; they are used for solemn occasions. And do not bring yellow flowers; yellow signifies hatred. If you're staying with a Bulgarian family, bring records, cassettes, jeans, or cigarettes purchased in the United States.

• Parker pens are popular business gifts.

Extras

• At hotels, leave your passport with the clerk if he asks for it and leave your key at the desk when you go out. Also, don't expect to take a bath whenever you feel like it. Signs are posted telling you

what time hot water is available.
- Make dinner reservations for the weekend several days in advance.
- German is the most widely spoken foreign language.

Czechoslovakia

Greetings
- Older people and women extend their hands in greeting first.
- At formal parties, don't talk with someone to whom you have not been introduced.
- Use professional titles, without last names, when speaking to doctors, lawyers, architects, or engineers.

Conversation
- Avoid political discussions.
- Czechoslovakians like to talk about sports, music, and family.

Public manners
- Gambling is forbidden.

Dress
- Jeans and shorts are acceptable casual wear.
- When dining in private homes or in small restaurants, men should wear pants and shirts, and women should wear dresses or skirts and blouses.
- For formal balls, operas, plays, and ballets, men should wear tuxedos. Women should wear gowns.

Table manners
- Wait until everyone has been served a drink before picking up your glass.
- Don't put your silverware down between bites.
- If you are offered a second helping, refuse politely, but when your hostess asks you again (which she will), accept politely.
- When you finish eating, place your utensils together at one side of the plate.

Private homes
- Sunday is visiting day. Call between 2 p.m and 5 p.m.

• If you're staying with a Czechoslovakian family, offer to do some of the shopping. Most people work, and lines are long at night when they must go shopping.

• If you eat at a private home, reciprocate by taking the family out to dinner at a restaurant.

Gifts

• If you're invited to dinner, bring cognac, wine, or whiskey.

• If you're staying with a family, bring American products: toys for the kids, make-up for the women, jeans, cigarette lighters, records, and T-shirts.

• Business gifts are unnecessary.

Extras

• Don't smoke while driving a car; it is illegal.

• Men should present flowers to a businesswoman when they first meet.

• At hotels, leave your passport at the desk when you check in. Leave your keys at the desk whenever you go out.

• No meat is served in restaurants on Thursdays.

• Restaurant rating is the opposite of American restaurant rating. The lower the numeral, the better the restaurant.

Denmark

Greetings

• Shake hands heartily when you meet someone you know.

Conversation

• Avoid personal topics, including income and religion.

• Don't give compliments.

Public manners

• People change into their bathing suits on the beach, using a towel as a cover.

Dress

• Casual wear consists of pants and sport shirts for men and pants and sweaters for women.

• Guests can wear jeans to casual dinners.

• At formal affairs, men should wear jackets and ties. Women should wear dresses or skirts and blouses.

Table manners

• Be punctual. Dinner is served immediately upon the guest's arrival.
• Don't taste the wine until the host makes the first toast.
• Before you taste your wine, glance around at everyone.
• During dessert, the man seated next to the hostess should propose a toast to her.
• You must take second helpings or you will insult your hostess.
• When finished, place your utensils, tines up, side by side, vertically on the plate.
• Don't get up until the hostess rises, and be sure to thank her for the dinner before she leaves the table.

Private homes

• If you're invited to a Danish home in the evening, do not assume that dinner is included.
• The Danes like to sit around the table and chat after a meal is finished.
• If you're staying with a Danish family, you will be expected to keep your room clean. You should also either take the family to dinner one night or prepare a dinner for them in their home.
• Instead of using the family's bath facilities daily, go to the public baths.

Gifts

• For dinner, bring liquor or flowers. The flowers should be wrapped. Bring flowers of the season or tiny roses.
• If you are staying with a Danish family that you know very well bring American products for gifts. Danish women will especially appreciate cosmetics, as they are very expensive in Denmark.
• Liquor is a good business gift.
• Don't give American cigarettes; Danes don't like them.

East Germany

Greetings

• When making introductions, always introduce younger people to older people and people of inferior social position to those of superior social position.

• When addressing a professional, use "Mr." or "Mrs." followed by the person's title.

Conversation

• Refer to the country as the German Democratic Republic.

• Avoid politics in conversation. Discuss families, professions, and sports.

Public manners

• Don't litter.

• Bargaining is considered impolite.

• Stand up when talking to women or social superiors.

• Avoid photographing anything.

Dress

• Shorts are unacceptable.

• Jeans are fine as casual wear.

• Businesspeople should wear conservative suits.

• Men do not need to wear jackets and ties when invited to dinner in a private home, but women should wear dresses.

• Wear formal clothing to weddings, the opera, or the theater. Men should wear dark suits and women short cocktail dresses (long dresses for the opera).

Table manners

• Always wait to be seated by your host or hostess.

• To indicate that you are merely taking a break, cross your utensils on your plate.

• When you are toasted, look at the wine and then at the toaster before drinking.

• When passing food to someone, always say "Bitte," which means in this case, "You're welcome."

• When finished, place your utensils parallel on the plate.

Gifts

• Bring flowers when you're invited to dinner and present them to your hostess unwrapped. Do not bring roses; they have romantic

implications.
- If you're visiting a family with a small child, bring a toy for the child.
- If you're staying with a German family, give American products as gifts.
- Give an unusual brand of whiskey as a business gift.

Extras
- Hotels will usually keep your passport for your entire stay, and the clerks expect you to leave your keys at the desk each time you go out.
- German businesspeople do not accept business appointments on Wednesdays.
- In restaurants, to get a waiter's attention, say "Herr Ober;" to get a waitress' attention, say "Fraulein."

Britain

Greetings
- To greet someone, shake his hand and say, "How do you do?" The person will respond with the same question, although neither of you will answer.
- Women should extend their hands first in greeting.
- Address surgeons as "Mr." not "Dr."
- Address members of the nobility or upper clergy by their correct titles.

Conversation
- First names are acceptable if used first by the British person in the group.
- Avoid political, social, and religious topics. Also, don't ask a lot of questions about a person's private life.
- If a conversation turns into an argument, remain as cool as your British opponent.
- Do not call a Scotsman or a Welshman "English."

Public manners
- Affection is not displayed in public.
- Do not stare at people or shout in public.

• Females should not be offended when called "love," "duckie,"
or "dearie."
• Stand during "God Save the Queen" no matter where you hear it.
• If you smoke, offer cigarettes to everyone in your group before
lighting up.
•Don't handle fruit and vegetables at market.

Dress
• Casual dress (even acceptable at some concerts and theater
performances) should be clean, neat jeans or tweeds.
• For restaurant dining, men should wear jackets and ties; women
should wear dresses or skirts and blouses.
• Avoid striped ties; they may be regimental colors.
• Formal wear can mean many things. Take the invitation to a formal shop. The staff there will tell you what you are expected to
wear.

Table manners
• It is polite to decline a second helping the first time it is offered.
• Ask before lighting a cigarette between courses.
• At dinner parties, don't smoke until after the queen has been
toasted at the end of the meal.
• At an upper-class dinner party, the women leave after the meal
so the men can smoke cigars and drink brandy.
• When the meal is over, place your utensils side by side on the
plate vertically.

Private homes
• If you're staying in a private home, keep your room tidy and
offer to help with the dishes.
• Ask your hostess what would be a convenient time to take a
bath; the British don't like to use too much hot water.

Gifts
• Bring flowers or wine if you're invited to dinner. Avoid white
lilies.
• Business gifts are not expected.

Extras

• Business dinners in Scotland are usually at a private home. Reciprocate with dinner at a restaurant.

• Businesswomen who are entertaining a male business associate should make arrangements to pay the maitre d' in advance.

• Once the day is over, don't discuss business; the British do not like to mix busines with pleasure.

• Double-deck buses are usually divided into two sections. Smokers should use the upper half.

Finland

Greetings

• Sometimes the Finns offer both hands to be shaken simultaneously.

• When introduced to a group containing children, shake their hands as well.

Conversation

• Avoid personal questions about family and profession, as well as the topic of Finnish neutrality.

Public manners

• Public affection is frowned upon.

• Wave at acquaintances you see in the distance.

• Men remove their hats when speaking to someone and when entering buildings and elevators.

• Smoking is forbidden in many public buildings.

• Don't fold your arms or prop your ankle up on the opposite knee; these gestures are considered impolite.

Dress

• Men are expected to wear suits and women dresses for business and dinner engagements.

• Men should wear tuxedos and women cocktail dresses to theater and opera openings.

Table manners

• Finns often invite people to coffee in the late afternoon. Sample each of the pastries offered or your hostess will be insulted.

- Don't start eating or leave the table before your host.
- Never toast the host or hostess.
- Don't drink until after the host has offered a toast.
- Don't eat anything with your hands.
- Thank the hostess immediately after dinner, even though you're expected to stay at least another hour.

Private homes

- If invited to take a family sauna, consider it a compliment.

Gifts

- If you want to give flowers as a dinner gift, pick a small bouquet of cut flowers.
- If you're staying with a family, bring American liquor or perfume as gifts.

Extras

- After a business deal is struck, you are expected to attend a long lunch followed by a sauna.
- Include spouses in invitations to business dinners.
- Heavy drinking is common at the dinner table.
- Do not get boisterous in public.
- Restaurant bills are never split. Whoever gave the invitation pays.

France

Greetings

- Shake children's hands as well as adults' hands.
- Don't use the last name in greeting; it is considered too casual. Use "Sir," "Madam," and "Miss."
- Friends and relatives kiss in greeting, once on each cheek

Conversation

- Avoid talking about prices, income, age, professions, and family; the French are very private.
- Dinner conversation is lively and expected.

Public manners

- Do not speak loudly in public or private.

- Don't chew gum in public.
- Do not handle market produce. Allow the vendors to choose for you.

Dress
- Casual dress should always be neat and clean.
- For the theater, men should wear dark suits and ties, and women should wear dresses.

Table manners
- Wait until the host has served wine to everyone and proposed a toast before you drink.
- The spoon and fork placed above the dinner plate are for dessert.
- Taste every dish.
- Don't smoke between courses.
- Don't use your bread to soak up the gravy or sauce on your plate.
- Peel and slice your fruit before eating it.
- When finished, place your utensils together with handles facing right and points up.

Private homes
- If you stay in a French home, do not take a daily or late night bath.
- Between meals, keep your napkin in the holder provided. The same napkin is used for several meals.
- If you're staying for several days, offer to do the dishes.

Gifts
- If you're invited to dinner, bring a box of chocolates or flowers other than chrysanthemums; they are used only for funerals.
- If you're staying with a French family, bring American products or books.
- Although business gifts are not expected, intellectually stimulating gifts are appreciated.

Extras
- Entertain French businesspeople by inviting them to dinner not lunch.
- Give your seat to elderly passengers on the bus or subway.

West Germany

Greetings

• Handshaking customs vary regionally. Take your cue from the Germans.
• Allow the host to introduce you at parties and business meetings.
• If you are introducing two people, introduce the younger or lower-ranking person first.
• Men should rise when a woman enters the room or when speaking to a standing woman.
• Women over 20 are addressed as "Frau."
• Use professional titles.
• Answer the phone using your last name.

Conversation

• Avoid personal questions and questions about World War II.
• Unlike most Europeans, Germans like to discuss politics.
• Do not give casual compliments. It will embarrass the Germans.

Public manners

• To attract someone's attention, raise your hand and extend your index finger.
• Never shout greetings.
• Public affection, including very toothy smiles, is frowned upon.
• Younger women should walk behind men into a restaurant.
• On the street, men always walk on the curb side of a woman.

Dress

• For dinner engagements, men should wear suits and women should wear dresses or skirts.
• Unless it is an opening night, in which case women should wear gowns, women should wear cocktail dresses and men suits to operas, concerts, and plays.

Table manners

• Don't drink until the host has taken his first drink.
• Women should never toast men.
• Never put your knife down during the meal or eat with your fingers.

• Do not use your knife to cut potatoes or dumplings; it will insult your hostess.
• Do not smoke between courses unless someone else has already lit up.
• When finished, lay your utensils together vertically on the plate.

Private homes
• If you're staying with a German family, always close room doors behind you.

Gifts
• If you're invited to dinner, bring an odd number (not 13) of uncut flowers for your hostess. Avoid red roses (romantic implications), large bouquets (ostentatious), and calla lilies (funeral flowers). You should either bring flowers unwrapped or unwrap them in the entrance way before giving them to your hostess. (Do not bring wine; your host will consider it an insult.)
• Bring American liquor, college sweatshirts, cassettes, and records for the family with whom you are staying. Avoid cosmetics and clothes.
• Packaging is very important. Do not use white, black, or brown paper.

Extras
• German hotels sometimes charge extra for access to the bathroom and for heat.
• In restaurants, address the waiter as "Herr Ober" and the waitress as "Fraulein."
• Don't ask for coffee with a meal; it is drank after the meal.
• Spouses are not included in business lunches.

Greece

Greetings
• Only close friends kiss each other in greeting.
• Do not address people by professional titles.

Conversation
• Avoid discussing Cyprus and American involvement in Greek affairs.

• Greeks like to discuss family, profession, and income; do not be offended.
• No is indicated by a raising of the head and eyebrows. An American No (a shake of the head from right to left) is an insult.

Public manners

• Be especially courteous to the elderly; they are well-respected and powerful.
• Do not wave with an open palm. Get someone's attention by gesturing with your index finger.
• Punctuality is unimportant in Greece.
• Bargaining is accepted in the local markets.

Dress

• Shorts are frowned upon.
• Formal wear consists of tuxedos for men and gowns for women.
• Women visiting churches should wear skirts and long-sleeved blouses.

Table manners

• Arrive 20 to 30 minutes late for a dinner engagement.
• The male guest of honor sits on the hostess' right. The female guest of honor sits on the host's right.
• Use the spoon above the plate for dessert.
• Watch your host to see what foods can be eaten with your fingers.
• Eat a lot to show you are pleased with the food.
• When finished, cross your fork (with tines down) on top of your knife.
• Stay after dinner until the conversation wanes.

Private homes

• Visiting starts about 5:30 p.m. Leave before dinner, or your hosts will feel obliged to invite you to join them.
• Don't compliment your host on a specific object; he will feel obliged to give it to you.
• If staying with a Greek family, find a way to include everyone in your plans.

- Ask before taking a bath and use little water.

Gifts

- Cut flowers are very expensive. Take wine or brandy to dinner.
- If you're staying with a family, bring American towels or mechanical products.
- If you're visiting or staying with a family that has children, you must bring toys for the children.
- Business gifts should be useful in an office—pens, paperweights, calculators.

Hungary

Greetings

- Address people by their professional titles followed by "Mr." or "Ms."
- If you're unsure of someone's professional title, address him by his last name, followed by "Mr." "Mrs." or "Miss."

Conversation

- Sudden changes in conversation are frequent due to the fear of saying too much.

Public manners

- On the street, a man should always walk to the left of a woman.

Dress

- For concerts and theater performances, men and women should wear business suits.
- For the opera, men should wear tuxedos; women should wear gowns.

Table manners

- After each course is served, wait for your hostess to start eating before beginning yourself.
- Guests should propose a toast to the host's health before drinking.
- Try your food before adding any seasonings, or you will insult your hostess.
- Do not cut your fish with a knife or your hostess will think her

food is undercooked.

Private homes
- Hungarian hosts will not accept offers to help with the housework if you're a houseguest.
- Hot water is available only in some apartments.

Gifts
- If you're invited to dinner, do not bring chrysanthemums. Any other flowers or American liquor are acceptable.
- If you're staying with a Hungarian family, bring American household items, cosmetics, or clothes as gifts.
- Business gifts are unnecessary. If you do want to give gifts, bring something for everyone, including the secretaries.

Extras
- The English pronunciation for the word "bus" means fornication in Hungarian. Pronounce the word "boos."
- Buckle your seat belt when you get in a taxi. The taxi driver will not drive if you do not.
- Business meetings are never held on Saturdays.
- There are no laundries in Hungary. You must wash your clothes in the bathtub.

Iceland

Greetings
- It is impolite to call an Icelander by his last name.

Gifts
- If you're invited to dinner in a private home, you should bring flowers or liquor to your host or hostess.

Extras
- Business appointments are unnecessary. Dropping in is the policy.

Ireland

Greetings
- Wait for a woman to extend her hand first.

- The Irish use only two occupational titles: doctor and professor.

Conversation
- Do not discuss Northern Ireland, women's rights, religion, or British policies toward Ireland.

Public manners
- Public displays of affection are frowned upon.
- The Irish change on the beach under towels.

Dress
- Most of the Irish wear dark tweeds or wools for casual clothes.
- Unless it's a business meal, men need not wear suits for a dinner party.
- Formal evening wear consists of tuxedos and cocktail dresses.

Table manners
- If you don't or can't drink alcohol, explain that it is for health reasons, or the Irish will be insulted.
- Raise your glass and say "Cheers" before taking a drink.
- Peel your potatoes before eating them. The Irish do not eat potato peelings.

Private homes
- Catholic houseguests are expected to attend Sunday mass with the family.
- Ask your hostess what would be a good time to bathe.

Gifts
- Dinner gifts could be flowers, chocolates, or cheeses.
- If someone gives you a gift, open it in front of him.
- Business gifts are not expected.

Extras
- Hitchhiking is common in Ireland. Call it being offered a seat. "Getting a ride" is obscene.
- Women are not allowed to buy rounds of drinks in pubs.

Italy

Greetings

- Kiss friends on each cheek.
- Greet male professionals with their occupational titles followed by their last names.
- Greet female professionals with *"Signora"* or *"Signorina"* followed by their occupational titles.

Conversation

- Avoid discussions about Italian politics. Italians like to discuss food, soccer, and family life.
- Don't ask new acquaintances about their occupations.

Public manners

- Stand when an older person enters the room and give up your seat on the bus to an older person.
- Ask before photographing someone. Do not photograph soldiers or military equipment.

Dress

- Even casual wear in Italy (jeans and slacks) is neat and elegant.
- For the opera or theater, men should wear conservative suits. Women should wear elegant short dresses.
- Opening nights require tuxedos and gowns.

Table manners

- Women do not pour wine.
- Drunkenness is offensive.
- Do not start eating until the hostess begins.
- The knife and fork above your plate are for peeling fruit. The spoon above your plate is for coffee or dessert.
- You probably will have three plates at your setting. The bottom one is for the main dish. The middle one is for the pasta dish. The top one is for the antipasto dish.
- Do not cut your pasta. Twirl it around your fork.
- Spear your cheese with a knife.
- Decline seconds politely. Allow the hostess to ask again.
- Don't smoke between courses.

- When finished, put the knife and fork together on the plate with the tines facing down.

Private homes
- Children are very important. If you visit an Italian home, be sure to pay attention to the children.
- If you're staying with a family, use your napkin sparingly. Italian families use the same napkin for several days.
- Ask your hostess what would be a convenient time to take a bath.

Gifts
- Dinner guests should bring a box of chocolates; a bouquet of an uneven number of flowers, other than chyrsanthemums, Italy's funeral flowers; or a few bottles of wine.
- If you stay with an Italian family, bring California wine or cigars and send some after you leave.
- In business, give gifts to anyone helpful to you. Give flowers to female business associates and pen sets or paperweights to male business associates.
- Never give brooches, hankerchiefs, or a set of knives as gifts. They signify mourning.

Extras
- Every time you leave your hotel, give the desk clerk your room key.
- Lone females should stay in first-class hotels.
- To attract a waiter, raise your hand and say *"Camariere"*; to attract a waitress, say *"Signorina."*
- In northern Italy, it is safe for women to eat alone, if they are especially careful about not looking at strange men.

The Netherlands

Greetings
- When introduced to someone, repeat your name as you shake his hand.
- If no one introduces you, introduce yourself. The Dutch will think you're rude if you do not.

Conversation

- Avoid discussing American politics and money. Talk about Dutch politics, artwork, and sports.
- Don't offer personal compliments unless you know someone well. (But the Dutch do like compliments on their home furnishings.)

Public manners

- Public affection is frowned upon.
- Do not chew gum or put your hands in your pockets when speaking to someone.
- Never interrupt salespeople if they are already helping someone else.
- Men should walk on the street side of a woman.
- Men should stand when a woman enters the room.

Dress

- Jeans are acceptable casual wear.
- Dress in suits or dresses for dinner in a Dutch home.
- On opening nights, men should wear tuxedos, and women should wear cocktail dresses. (On other nights, suits and dresses are fine.)

Table manners

- Do not start eating until after the hostess has taken the first bite.
- Taste everything offered to you.
- The dessert spoon is above the plate.
- Getting up during a meal is considered very rude.
- Most households allow you to smoke between courses.

Private homes

- If you're staying with a Dutch family, keep your room neat and offer to help with the dishes.

Gifts

- Unwrapped flowers are the best dinner gift.
- Don't bring wine. The Dutch have their own wine cellars.
- If you're staying with a family, bring best-selling books or American T-shirts. Be sure to bring the children gifts.

Extras

- Use the correct titles in business dealings.
- Dutch businessmen do not mind when foreign businesswomen pay for the meal in restaurants.
- The Dutch do not like spontaneous decisions. Plan business meetings well in advance.
- Women should avoid Zeedyk Street in Amsterdam. Prostitutes sit in the shop windows.

Norway

Greetings

- Professors, doctors, and engineers should be addressed by their occupational titles followed by their last names. Lawyers and clergymen should be addressed by their last names only.
- Men are commonly addressed by their last names.

Conversation

- Avoid personal questions and criticisms. Norwegians like to talk about politics, sports, and hobbies.

Public manners

- Public affection and loud voices are frowned upon.
- Let a public attendant clean the stall before using a public bathroom.

Dress

- Jeans and T-shirts are fine for casual wear.
- If invited to someone's home for dinner, men should wear suits, and women should wear dresses, skirts, or dressy pantsuits.
- In larger restaurants, men must wear jackets and ties.
- Dress formally for openings. Men should wear dark suits, and women should wear cocktail dresses.

Table manners

- Do not start eating until your host or hostess begins.
- Dinner lasts several hours.
- Most homes allow you to smoke between courses. Ask.
- When finished eating, cross your utensils in the middle of your plate.

Private homes

- In the countryside you need not call before you visit someone. Late afternoon is reserved for visitors.
- Bring some type of pastry when you're invited to coffee.
- Norwegian families expect their guests to offer to clear the table after meals if they are staying for a few days. It is only a matter of form. They will decline your offer.

Gifts

- Flowers and liquor are appropriate dinner gifts. Do not bring white flowers, carnations, or wreaths. They are used in funerals.
- Houseguests should bring regional products from their home states, American liquor, or frozen beef. (Meat is very expensive in Norway.) Steak is be greatly appreciated.

Poland

Greetings

- Polish men sometimes kiss the hands of American women in greeting.
- Use a person's professional title when speaking to him.

Conversation

- The Poles like to hear about life in the United States. They may ask you intimate details about your life.
- Polish men respond better to quiet, subtle women than direct, outspoken women.

Public manners

- Don't walk on the grass. It is illegal in many areas.
- Bargain only in open markets.
- Women should ask another woman for directions if they get lost. If they ask a man, they will be considered flirtatious.

Dress

- Jeans are fine for casual wear.
- For business meetings and restaurant dining, men wear suits, and women wear dresses.
- Women should not wear revealing dresses to church.
- If formal wear is specified on an invitation, men should wear

tuxedos, and women should wear gowns.

Table manners
- If you are toasted during a meal, return the toast later with "To your health."
- Wait until everyone has been served before you begin to eat.
- A Pole invites you for a drink by flicking his finger against his neck.
- When beet soup is served, you are expected to drink from the bowl.
- When you are finished eating, leave a little food on your plate or your hostess will refill your plate.
- Do not leave a dinner party early or you will insult your host.

Private homes
- Sunday is visiting day, but call first.
- Ask before taking a bath. Your host will have to heat the water.

Gifts
- A bouquet of an uneven number of flowers is the best dinner gift. Do not bring chrysanthemums; they are funeral flowers.
- If you're a houseguest, buy your hosts something from the "dollar stores" that accept only foreign currency. The Poles especially like fruit, hams, and cognac.
- If you bring gifts from the United States, bring cigarettes, whiskey, or coffee.
- Bring American whiskey or cognac as a business gift.

Extras
- Give the desk clerk your passport to keep during your stay and your room key every time you go out.
- In hotels, you can get extra towels from the attendant stationed on your floor.

Portugal

Greetings
- Close male friends embrace. Close female friends kiss on both cheeks.
- Professional titles are used before last names for doctors,

professors, engineers, and lawyers.

Conversation
- Avoid personal questions about income and profession. Discuss families, hobbies, sports, and wine.

Public manners
- Avoid public affection.
- Show respect for the elderly.
- You can bargain in craft shops.
- Don't buy food from street vendors.

Dress
- For business meetings and dinner engagements, men should wear suits. Women should wear dresses and high heels.
- Theater and opera openings require tuxedos for men and dark dresses for women.

Table manners
- Don't start eating a course of a meal until everyone has been served.
- At a family dinner, the guest is served first, and then the older people.
- Always keep your napkin on your lap and never eat with your hands.
- Don't smoke between courses.
- Don't use bread to soak up the gravy on your plate.
- When finished, fold your napkin.

Private homes
- Never follow your hostess into the kitchen unless specifically invited.

Gifts
- You don't have to bring a dinner gift when invited to dinner. However, it is a nice gesture if you take your hosts out to dinner in return another night.
- If you do bring a dinner gift, bring chocolates. Never bring wine because most people have wine cellars, of which they are very proud.

- If you are a houseguest, bring American handicrafts or books about the United States.
- Before coming to Portugal, ask your Portuguese business associates what gifts they would like you to bring them.

Extras

- If your business associates offer you a drink, accept.
- Women should take taxis after 8 p.m. rather than walk.
- If you are invited to the cinema, dress in suits and dresses; the Portuguese consider this a social event.

Romania

Greetings

- Romanian men usually kiss the hands of foreign women.
- Good friends of the same sex often exchange kisses.
- Call professionals by their occupational titles followed by their last names.

Conversation

- Romanians tend to be formal with foreigners.
- Avoid discussions about communism and the U.S.S.R. Do not ask new acquaintances questions about their families or jobs.
- Romanians are very interested in the arts—music, drama, fashion, books. These are safe subjects as long as they are not about controversial topics.

Public manners

- Be careful about what you photograph.
- Carry toilet paper with you. There is none in the public bathrooms.

Dress

- Jeans are acceptable casual wear.
- For business, men should wear dark suits, white ties, and well-polished shoes. Women should wear suits and high heels.
- Formal wear is unnecessary. Suits and dresses are worn in restaurants.

Table manners

- Keep your napkin on the table.
- Toast your host's health several times during a meal.
- Sample everything on your plate.

Private homes

- Romanian families must report your arrival to the local police, so do not stop in without prior notice.
- If you're staying with a Romanian family, it is polite to offer to help with the housework.
- Check with your hostess to find out what is a convenient time for you to take a bath.

Gifts

- Wrapped flowers are appropriate as a dinner gift.
- If you're staying with a Romanian family, bring coffee, cosmetics, or clothes for each member of the family.
- Inexpenive pens, letter openers, or lighters are the best business gifts.

Spain

Greetings

- Although an older or higher ranking individual may call you by your first name, you must call him by his last name.
- In writing use both , the surname and the mother's maiden name. In conversation, use only the surname.

Conversation

- Use family names and professional titles until you become better acquainted.
- Avoid personal questions until you become better acquainted. Discuss soccer, the Spanish countryside, or life in the United States.
- Avoid the topic of bullfighting.

Public manners

- It is fashionable to be late.
- The Spanish tend to interrupt speakers frequently; this is not considered rude.

- Do not use the "Okay" sign; it is a vulgar gesture in Spain.
- Men and women often use the same public bathrooms.
- Women should not make eye contact with men; they will be approached if they do.
- Do not take pictures of military equipment or soldiers.

Dress
- Women should never wear pants for business meetings. They should wear dresses. Men should wear suits.
- Formal wear consists of tuxedos and gowns.
- Men should wear conservative suits and black shoes to dinner engagements. Women should wear dresses or skirts.

Table manners
- The utensils above your plate are for dessert.
- Butter is served only with bread at breakfast.
- Spaniards are not pushy about second servings. If you don't want seconds, say so.
- When finished, leave your knife and fork side by side on the plate. If you leave them on opposite ends, you are implying that you weren't satisfied with the meal.

Private homes
- Late afternoon is the best time to visit a Spanish home.
- If you are invited to visit a Spanish home (a real honor) stay at least two hours, or your hosts will think you are rude.
- Do not ignore the children. They are very important members of the family.
- If you are staying with a Spanish family, they will expect to spend the entire day with you. Be tactful if you wish to be alone.
- Do not snack between meals.
- Do not take a bath without asking; hot water must be heated.

Gifts
- Bring flowers or chocolates as a dinner gift. Avoid dahlias and chrysanthemums.
- If you're staying in a Spanish home, bring American products as gifts—whites (sheets), quilts, electronic equipment, jeans, or toys.
- If the family you are staying with has children, buy them toys

or candy when you go sightseeing.

• If you are given a gift, open it immediately.

Extras

• Offices, banks, and schools are closed from about 2 p.m. to 4 p.m. everyday for siesta.

• Business relations are very formal. You should establish a business contact through a Spanish intermediary. Don't talk business on the first meeting. And you should not force Spaniards to speed up the pace of the transaction; you will offend their honor.

• In hotels, leave your key at the desk every time you go out.

• Women should take a taxi after dark.

Sweden

Greetings

• Use professional titles when addressing Swedes.

• Younger people are less formal. They do not expect you to shake their hands every time you see them, nor do they expect you to use their professional titles when addressing them.

• The older members of the upper class speak of themselves in the third person. Respect this habit.

Conversation

• When you see someone who has recently invited you for dinner, be sure to say "Thank you for last time" immediately.

• Eye contact is appreciated.

• The Swedes like to talk about their country. Any knowledge you have of Sweden is noted and appreciated.

• Avoid criticism of Sweden. No country likes to hear about the negative aspects of its culture and history.

• Do not give casual compliments. Only good friends exchange compliments.

Public manners

• Men should always raise their hats when passing an acquaintance on the street and remove their hats when speaking to a woman.

- Public affection is not displayed.

Dress
- Do not wear informal clothes at any time. You will be very much out of place.
- Formal wear consists of tuxedos for men and short cocktail dresses for women. (Women should not wear black.)

Table manners
- Try every dish you are offered.
- At formal dinners, you will be supplied with a special butter knife. Do not use your dinner knife for butter.
- Do not toast your host or anyone older than you until he toasts you first.
- When you are toasted, do not drink your drink until the person toasting you has said *"skoal."*
- To toast someone properly, you must bring your glass up to eye level, look directly into that person's eyes, say *"skoal,"* drink your drink in one gulp, make a slight flourish with your hand toward the person you are toasting, then lower your glass to the table.
- Never toast the hostess when there are more than six people at the table. Everyone would have to toast her then, and she would be forced to drink quite a bit. If you do toast the hostess, toast her with a simple "Thank you."
- Call the next day to thank your host and hostess for the dinner.

Private homes
- An invitation to a private home in the evening is not an invitation to dinner. An invitation to dinner is very specifically stated.

Gifts
- If you're invited to dinner, bring your hostess a bouquet of unwrapped flowers or a bottle of liquor.
- If you're staying with a Swedish family, bring American books or records. Do not bring objects for which Sweden is famous; it is an insult.
- American liquor is an appropriate business gift.

Extras

- Speaking with your hands is considered impolite.
- Business dinners and lunches are very popular. Make reservations several days in advance.
- Drive with your headlights on at all times.

Switzerland

Greetings

- Greeting habits differ from region to region. In the French region, female friends embrace and kiss each other on each cheek. Men in this region embrace only when they haven't seen each other for a long time. In the Italian region, women embrace but do not kiss each other. Men embrace only if they haven't seen each other for a long time. In the German region, people show less public signs of affection. Only women friends who haven't seen each other in a long time embrace. Everyone else shakes hands.

Conversation

- The Swiss are more formal than the Swedes. Use last names when addressing people.
- Avoid delving into someone's personal life—income, family, occupation. The Swiss like to talk about politics, sports, and culture.

Public manners

- If you see someone you know at a distance, you need not stop to talk, just call out "Hello."
- Help the elderly if they seem to need help.
- Bargaining is considered impolite.
- Poor posture is frowned upon.

Dress

- The Swiss do not approve of shorts in the city.
- If you're invited to dinner in a Swiss home, men should wear nice pants and sweaters, and women should wear skirts or nice pantsuits.
- Formal wear consists of tuxedos and gowns.

Table manners

• Do not drink until your host has toasted the party. You then raise your glass, look at the host, and say "To your health" in the appropriate language. (Clink glasses with everyone.)
• The dessert spoon will be at the top of your plate.
• Don't smoke between courses.
• If you want a second helping, cross your fork over your knife, tines facing left and point facing right.
• When finished, place your knife and fork horizontally across the plate, pointing to the right.

Private homes

• If you're staying with a Swiss family, keep your room neat and clean.
• The Swiss use the same napkin for several meals. Use your napkin sparingly and keep it in the ring provided between meals.

Gifts

• Flowers or candy are appropriate dinner gifts. Small bouquets are best. Do not bring chrysanthemums, white asters, red roses, or carnations. If you bring candy, make sure it is expensive and nicely packaged.
• House guests should bring distinctly American gifts and chocolates for the children.
• A bottle of American whiskey is appropriate as a business gift.

Extras

• In the German section, businessmen are very straightforward. In the French and Italian sections, businessmen are more subtle. They will engage you in some opening small talk.
• You do not need to leave your room key at the desk when you go out.
• The Swiss do not normally order drinks before a meal, and will consider it strange if you do.

Turkey

Greetings
• When you enter a room, shake hands with everyone present,

starting with the eldest. You do not have to shake hands again when you leave.

• Always show respect to the older members of society. Rise when they enter a room.

• The Turks use first names when addressing each other in social situations. Call men by their first names followed by *"bay."* Call women by their first names followed by *"hanim."*

• When you address a male professional, use his occupational title alone. For a female professional, you should use her occupational title followed by *"bayan."*

Conversation

• Never cross your arms or put your hands in your pockets when speaking to someone; it is rude.

• When seated do not cross your legs. Showing the soles of your feet is disrespectful.

• Turks like to talk about their families and occupations. Avoid discussions about Cyprus, Greece, or communism.

• Turkish men are especially pleased if you ask about their sons.

• Always allow your elders to speak first in a conversation and never raise your voice to them.

• When someone raises his chin and shuts his eyes, he is saying "No."

• To get someone's attention, move your hand up and down, not side to side.

Public manners

• Do not touch members of the opposite sex in public.

• Remove your shoes when you visit a mosque.

• Stand up quietly when the national anthem is played.

• Ask permission before taking anyone's picture. It is against the Islamic faith to reproduce the human image.

• Bargain for everything. Start at a quarter of the real value.

Dress

• Do not wear shorts even for casual wear.

• Women should always dress modestly. Dresses should be over the knee or longer. Do not wear low-cut or backless dresses.

• Women should cover their heads and wear long-sleeved

garments when visiting a mosque.
* Formal dress is seldom used. It consists of tuxedos and gowns.

Table manners
* Never eat with your fingers.
* The Turks respect a healthy appetite. You will offend them if you do not eat heartily.
* Don't smoke between courses unless others at your table light up.
* When you are offered Turkish coffee, you must specify if you want it sweet, medium, or without sugar.
* After dinner, say *"Ziyade olsun"* to your hostess. This means "Thank you for the energy you've spent."

Private homes
* Most guests visit about 9 p.m.
* Turks, even casual acquaintances, like to invite Americans home for a lengthy visit. If you want to refuse, tell them you already have arrangements.
* If your host offers you cologne, pour it into your hands and rub it on your face and hands.
* Do not make long-distance phone calls. The family cannot accept payment, even though they may not be able to afford to pay the bill.
* If you are staying several days, insist on helping with the household chores.

Gifts
* Roses, carnations, and candy are appropriate dinner gifts.
* If you're staying with a family, bring American crafts or books for the adults and candy or toys for the children.
* A Turkish hostess will not open your gift in front of you; it is considered rude. Do not be offended.
* Give American whiskey as a business gift if you know that your contact drinks. If not, give him a pen set or a book in English about his sphere of business.

Extras
* Bargain taxi fare with drivers before you get into the taxi.

- If you invite someone to a meal, you must pay the entire check. If someone else invites you to a meal, he will pay the entire check.
- Stay at a first-class hotel. If you stay at anything less, you will be disturbed by the noise.
- Driving is hazardous. There are no rules about who has the right of way.

Yugoslavia

Greetings
- Yugoslavs usually embrace and kiss friends in greeting.
- When addressing professionals, use their titles.

Conversation
- Yugoslavs do not mind personal questions and feel no compunction about asking you personal questions. They are also interested in life in the United States.
- Avoid political and ideological issues unless the conversation is initiated by a Yugoslav.

Public manners
- Yugoslavs promenade through town every evening between 5 p.m. and 8 p.m. to mingle with friends.
- Ask for permission before you photograph anything, including people.

Dress
- Jeans are usually worn only by young adults and teenagers.
- Dress in cities tends to be more formal, especially for women, who commonly wear dresses.
- In the late afternoon, after a nap at home, Yugoslavs generally walk around in sleepwear.
- When visiting churches, women should wear long-sleeved dresses. Men should wear suits.
- Businesswomen tend to dress in very fashionable suits and wear heels and a lot of make-up.
- Formal wear consists of gowns and dark suits.

Table manners
- Yugoslavs serve large amounts of food at dinner parties. It is

Dining in Europe

Country	Breakfast (a.m.)	Lunch (p.m.)	Dinner (p.m.)	Additional Information
Austria	8:00	1:00	7:00 to 9:00	Both dinner and lunch are substantial.
Belgium	7:30	12:00	7:00 to 8:00	In the country, lunch is the main meal.
Britain	7:30 to 8:30	12:00 to 3:00	7:00	Breakfast is a big meal. Dinner parties start at 8 p.m. The British have tea every day at 3:30 p.m. to 4:30 p.m.
Bulgaria	6:30 or 7:30	1:00	8:00	
Czechoslovakia	6:00	12:00 to 1:00	5:30 to 6:30	Lunch is usually the main meal of the day.
Denmark	8:00	12:00 to 3:00	6:00 to 8:00	Sandwiches are popular at lunch and dinner.
East Germany	8:00 to 9:00	12:00 to 1:00	6:00 to 7:00	Lunch is the main meal of the day.
Finland	7:30 to 9:00	12:00 to 1:00	5:00 or 6:00	Dinner is the main meal of the day.
France	7:00 to 8:00	12:00 to 2:30	7:00 to 9:30	Lunch is the main meal of the day.
Greece	7:00	1:30 to 2:00	8:30 to 9:30	Lunch or dinner could be the main meal.
Hungary	8:00 to 9:00	1:00 to 2:00	7:00 to 8:00	Lunch is the main meal of the day.
Ireland	8:00 to 10:00	1:00 to 2:00	5:00 to 8:00	Lunch or dinner could be the main meal.
Italy	8:00	1:00	8:00	Lunch is the main meal.
Luxembourg	7:30	12:00	7:00 or 8:00	Lunch is the main meal in the country.
The Netherlands	7:30	1:00	6:00	Lunch is the main meal in rural areas.
Norway	8:30	12:00	5:00 to 6:00	Dinner is the main meal.
Poland	7:00 or 8:00	3:00 to 4:00	8:00 to 9:00	The Poles eat lunch when they get home from work.
Portugal	7:30 to 8:00	12:00 to 2:00	7:30 to 8:00	Both lunch and dinner are large.
Romania	6:00 or 7:00	12:00	7:00 to 7:30	Lunch is the main meal. Dinner is leftovers.
Spain	7:00 to 8:00	2:00 to 3:00	9:00 to 10:00	Lunch is the main meal.
Sweden	7:00 or 8:00	12:00 to 1:00	5:00	Lunch is usually the main meal.
Switzerland	7:00	12:00	6:00 or 7:00	Lunch is the main meal.
Turkey	7:30 or 8:00	12:00	7:00	Breakfast is fairly large.
West Germany	7:00 to 8:30	1:00	6:30 to 7:30	Lunch is usually the main meal.
Yugoslavia	8:00	2:00	9:00	Lunch is usually the main meal. Dinner is leftovers.

polite to taste every dish.
- If you do not drink alcoholic beverages, you must give some kind of explanation or your hosts will be offended.
- When finished, place your utensils side by side completely on the plate, or your host will think you are merely taking a break.

Private homes
- The usual visiting hour is 5 p.m.
- Accept refreshments during a visit, or you will offend your hosts.
- If you're staying with a family, shake hands when you rise and again when you retire.
- Bathing everyday is understood, but washing your hair everyday is considered harmful.

Gifts
- If you're invited to dinner, bring American coffee, whiskey, or chocolates as a gift. If you did not bring these products into Yugoslavia with you, take flowers to dinner.
- If you're staying with a Yugoslav family, bring gifts made in America—cosmetics, clothes, regional crafts, or cigarettes.
- A gift with your company logo on it is an appropriate business gift.

Extras
- There is a significant Moslem community in Yugoslavia. When it celebrates Ramadan, many businesses and restaurants are closed.

TIPPING

There is no worldwide rule about tipping, so it's easy to make a mistake. The following is a European tipping chart that should help you through your trip:

Tips on Tipping

Country	Taxi	Restaurant	Hotel
Austria	15%	none	none
Belgium	15%	none	none
Denmark	none	none	none
France	15%	none	concierge: FF150 for extra service
Great Britain	10%	coffeeshop: 10% restaurant: none	none
Greece	10%	none	none
Italy	3% to 7% in addition to service charge	none	none
The Netherlands	none	none	none
Portugal	10%	none	none
Scandinavian Countries	10%	none	none
Spain	none	5% to 10% in addition to service charge	5% to 10% in addition to service charge
West Germany	none	none	none

MISCELLANEOUS

Emergency telephone numbers

European countries have emergency telephone numbers. They are usually listed in the front of the local telephone book. (Note, they do not work in some rural areas.)

Austria—*144* ambulance, *133* police.
Belgium—*900* or *901*.
Bulgaria—*166* police, *150* ambulance, *160* fire.
Czecholoslovakia—*158* police, *150* ambulance.
East Germany—*110* police, *112* fire, *115* ambulance.
France—Local number of the Brigade de Gendarmerie.
Great Britain—*999*.
Greece—*100* police, *525555* ambulance.
Hungary—*07* police, *04* ambulance.
Ireland—Local number of Garda.
Italy—*113*.
Luxembourg—*012*.
Monaco—*93304246* police, *93300485* ambulance.
Norway—*331290* police, *201090* ambulance.
Portugal—*115*.
Spain—*091* (Barcelona and Madrid).
Sweden—*90000*.
Switzerland—*17, 117, 11, 12, 111, 112*.
The Netherlands—*222222*.
West Germany—*110*.
Yugoslavia—*92* police, *94* ambulance.

European road service

Austria. Emergency phones are placed at one-mile intervals along all major highways.
Belgium. Call the local number for the Touring Secours VAB-BTB (Wacht op de Weg).
Denmark. Call the local number for Forenede Danske Motorejere.
Finland. Go to or call the nearest filling station.
France. Call the local number for the Police Secours-assistance.

Germany. Call the local number for the Strassenwacht.

Great Britain. Use the phones placed at one-mile intervals on main highways. Call *01-262-2638*.

Greece. Call *107*.

Ireland. Go to or call the nearest filling station.

Italy. If you're stranded on the autostrade, use the phones placed at one-mile intervals and call the Soccorso autostradale. On other roads, call *113* and ask for Soccorso autostradale.

Luxembourg. Call *311031* and ask for the Secours automobile.

Netherlands. Call the local number for Wegenwacht.

Norway. Call the local number for Norges Automobile Forbund from June through September.

Portugal. Go to or call the nearest filling station.

Spain. Go to or call the nearest filling station.

Sweden. Call the local number for Larmtjonst AB.

Switzerland. Use the emergency phones placed at one-mile intervals on the main highways.

Yugoslavia. Go to or call the nearest filling station.

U.S. embassies

American embassies can provide aid to American travelers and residents in the following situations:

If you are robbed, assualted, or arrested while abroad, contact the consul or ask that the consul be contacted if you are unable to do so. If you've been arrested, the consul will visit you to make sure your conditions are satisfactory. The consul can also contact your relatives and find you legal representation.

If you require medical assistance, the consul can help you find an English-speaking doctor, inform relatives or friends of your situation, and help you locate funds to pay for the services (although the consul will not advance you the money).

If you are involved in a legal dispute, the consul can provide you with a list of local lawyers and inform you of your rights as an American citizen. If you or a companion dies while abroad, the embassy can arrange for shipping of the body.

If your passport is stolen or expires while abroad, the embassy can replace it for the customary fee ($42).

If your passport is stolen or expires while abroad, the embassy can replace it for the customary fee ($42).

If local social upheaval occurs, the embassy can provide protection and assistance. (As soon as you enter a high-risk area, you should register with the consul so that you can be located in an emergency.)

If you have received serious terrorist threats, the embassy can provide you with some type of protection.

Do not expect much help if you go against the local authorities wishes. It is the embassy's job to maintain good public relations with their hosts. In these cases, individual American needs are secondary concerns.

Money

Exchange American currency only at official places—banks, airports, or foreign exchange offices. Deak International recommends that you exchange about $200 worth of money into local currency for each country you plan to visit. Never exchange more than $300. Before you exchange your money, make sure no one is watching you or sees the amount you pocket. When you leave, make sure no one follows you.

Customs

Every country has customs regulations and the United States is no exception. Upon your return you must fill out the proper forms if you are to make it through customs quickly and easily. The following is a brief outline of customs restrictions and exclusions:

If you have spent less than $400 on imports, you are exempt from customs duties, unless you have been out of the country for less than 48 hours or you have already used this exemption within the last 30 days. (Otherwise the exemption is only $25.)

Cigarettes and liquor are part of the $400 exemption as long as you have less than 100 cigars or 200 cigarettes and less than one liter (about two pints) of alcohol. Otherwise, hard liquor will be taxed at 10% (wine and beer is taxed at a little less). (Perfume also has restrictions.)

$5,000 in money, checks, or negotiable goods must be reported to customs (in both foreign and domestic currencies).

Restricted items include drugs, artworks or artifacts, and most animals and fish. Prohibited items include illegal drugs, absinthe, hard liquor exceeding the toxic level established by the government, most agricultural products, endangered species and articles made from their bodies, pornographic publications, all primates, lottery tickets, items made from forced labor, and books, records, and cassettes that violate copyright laws.

For a complete listing of restrictions, exemptions, and prohibitions, contact the **U.S. Customs Service,** *P.O. Box 7118, Washington, DC 20044.* Request the *Know Before You Go* brochure, publication number 512.

International telephone calls

The following chart can help you place telephone calls to European countries:

Country	Time Difference (New York)	Country Codes
Andorra	6 hours	33
Austria	6 hours	43
Belgium	6 hours	32
Bulgaria	7 hours	call operator for assistance
Canary Islands	5 hours	34
Cyprus	7 hours	357
Czechoslovakia	6 hours	42
Denmark	6 hours	45
East Germany	6 hours	37
England	5 hours	44
Finland	7 hours	358
France	6 hours	33
Gibraltar	6 hours	call operator for assistance
Greece	7 hours	30
Greenland	2 hours	call operator for assistance
Hungary	6 hours	36

Country	Time Difference (New York)	Country Codes
Iceland	5 hours	354
Ireland	5 hours	353
Isle of Man	5 hours	44
Italy	6 hours	39
Liechtenstein	6 hours	41
Luxembourg	6 hours	352
Madeira Islands	5 hours	351
Monaco	6 hours	33
Netherlands	6 hours	31
Northern Ireland	5 hours	44
Norway	6 hours	31
Poland	6 hours	48
Portugal	6 hours	351
Romania	7 hours	40
San Marino	6 hours	39
Scotland	5 hours	44
Spain	6 hours	34
Sweden	6 hours	46
Switzerland	6 hours	41
Turkey	7 hours	90
U.S.S.R.	8 hours (Moscow)	call operator for assistance
Wales	5 hours	44
West Germany	6 hours	49
Yugoslavia	6 hours	38

Chapter 3

Festivals

January 1: New Year's Day

In 153 B.C., the Romans designated January 1 the beginning of the new year. However, in the Middle Ages, the Christians changed the first day of the year to December 25 (to coincide with Jesus' birthday), and then to March 25 (the Feast of the Annunciation). Finally, in the 16th century, Pope Gregory XIII returned the celebration of the new year to January 1.

New Year's Day is celebrated in every country throughout Europe. Most families bring in the new year by visiting relatives and friends, then coming home for a celebration dinner. In **England** and **Scotland**, wassail (from the Gaelic *was hael,* meaning *good health*) bowls are used to drink a toast to the new year.

Throughout **Greece**, January 1 is also the **Feast of St. Basil**, patron saint of the Greek Orthodox Church. On this day children go from door to door, carrying an apple and a paper ship or star. They are given coins in return for singing carols of good wishes. According to Byzantine tradition, the *vasilopita* (New Year's cake) is sliced on this day. If you get the piece with the coin baked inside, you can look forward to a year of good fortune.

As January 1 marks the beginning of a fresh new year and a clean slate, many see it as a day for resolutions. This practice of making promises for the coming year was begun by the Romans, who hoped to please the god Janus with vows of good conduct.

January 6: Epiphany

Epiphany (literally "appearance" or "manifestation of the Son of God to man") celebrates the night 12 days after Jesus' birth

when the Three Wise Men arrived in Bethlehem. In many
countries, Epiphany is known as Three Kings' Day.

In **Sweden**, **Austria**, and **Switzerland**, young people dress as
the Magi and parade through the streets singing carols and
carrying a banner decorated with a star of Bethlehem.

The traditional blessing of the waters takes place in **Piraeus,
Greece**. A cross is thrown into the water by the local priest. The
diver who retrieves it is blessed with good luck for the coming
year.

In **Spain**, this is a big day for the country's children. Known as
the Cabalgatas de los Reyes Magos (Feast of the Three Kings), it
is the day when the little ones get their Christmas presents. The
arrival of the Magi the night before is re-enacted in a parade that
begins at 5 p.m. behind the town hall in Malaga. The parade's 500
participants ride on colorful floats accompanied by people dressed
as Roman soldiers, Arab merchants, Galician shepherds, and
music groups. Passengers on the floats toss five tons of candy to
the children along the route.

Epiphany is also the day when children in **Rome** receive their
presents. Befana (the gift-bearing witch) swoops down to leave
goodies in children's stockings. (She only leaves presents, though,
if a child has remembered to fill his stocking with *carbone finto*, a
hunk of black spun sugar.)

In **France**, each family buys a cake called the *galette du roi*
(tart of the king) for the Epiphany celebration. The cake has a coin
baked inside. Whoever gets the piece with the coin is crowned
king or queen for the day.

January 17: Fiesta de San Antonio

St. Anthony was born in Egypt in A.D. 251 and spent most of
his life praying and fasting in the desert. He was tempted many
times by the devil, who appeared to him in the form of a woman.
Since the Middle Ages, he has been acknowledged as the patron
saint of domestic animals.

In **Spain**, the Fiesta de San Antonio was originally celebrated with the blessing of the town's animals. Today, the people no longer take their livestock to the church for the local priest to bless with holy water. Instead, they celebrate the day with feasts and parties. The day is especially important in many Andalusian towns, including Maro and Mijas. In Mijas, villagers make a pilgrimage to the San Antonio monastery, where unmarried girls in search of husbands can improve their chances by throwing pebbles at the saint's image.

On the eve of the Feast of St. Antonio, huge *foguerons* (bonfires) light up the streets, and costumed dancers and singing groups roam through the towns. In Catalonia and the Balearic Islands, traditional mounted processions take place. In Ciudad Real bread and rolls are blessed. And Barcelona celebrates with a performance of the 17th-century "Ball del Ciri" (Candle Dance).

Last week of January: Mozart Week

This week in honor of Wolfgang Amadeus Mozart features symphonic concerts, chamber music, sacred music, and instrumental recitals. Most of the performances take place at the Mozarteum in Mozart's birthplace, **Salzburg, Austria**.

Late January: Elfstedentocht

Young men in the northern province of Friesland in **the Netherlands** have always tried to skate over the frozen canals that connect the province's 11 towns. In the 18th century, some boys tried to skate over all the canals in one day. Today, when it is cold enough, thousands of skaters race the same 124-mile course in what has become known as the Eleven Cities Race.

February 2: Candlemas

The purification of the Virgin Mary and Jesus' first appearance in the temple are commemorated throughout Catholic Europe on this day. During the celebrations, cowbells ring ceaselessly, and the "devils" (townspeople) run and jump through the streets, raising their arms as they stare at statues of Mary and the Christ Child. Turtledoves, candles (portending a good year if they remain lit, a bad one if they go out), and large cakes play important roles in the festivities, as do candlelight processions.

February 14: St. Valentine's Day

This celebration of love dates back to Roman times, when, during the Feast of Lupercus (the god of fertility), young men drew the names of young women who became their companions for the remainder of the year.

The feast acquired its present-day name in A.D. 270, when St. Valentine, a Roman priest, was imprisoned for conducting illegal marriage ceremonies. During his imprisonment, St. Valentine fell in love with his jailor's daughter. Before he was executed on Feb. 14, he wrote a farewell note to his beloved, which he signed, "Your Valentine."

By the 14th century, heart-shaped cards were popular in Great Britain, and men were giving presents to their sweethearts on this day. The first commercial cards appeared by 1800.

Late February to mid-March: Carnival

The day before Lent (the 40-day period of abstinence that ends with Easter) is a time for celebration throughout Europe. Mardi Gras, as the day is known, began as a pagan ritual of spring but eventually became tied to the Christian holiday of Easter.

Mardi Gras, or Fat Tuesday (the day always falls on a Tuesday), is a time of feasting. The day before Lent is also known as Shrove Tuesday, because originally people went to church on this day to confess, or shrive, their sins.

In the Middle Ages, Lent meant no butter, meat, or eggs. So on Fat Tuesday, everyone tried to use up all the butter, meat, and eggs in his kitchen, usually by making pancakes. This tradition is remembered in **Olney, England** with a pancake race that dates back to 1445. According to the legend, a housewife was making pancakes when the shriving bell rang. She rushed to church with her skillet in her hand. Her run is repeated every year during the race. Each woman who participates must flip a pancake three times while racing.

In **Luxembourg** the day before Lent is known as Pretzel Sunday. Boys offer their sweethearts pretzels as signs of their love. If the girl wishes to accept the boy's love, she takes the pretzel and returns an egg. The exchange is followed by a parade and all-night dancing.

Throughout the centuries, Mardi Gras has become known not only as the last chance to eat before Lent, but also as the last chance to have fun. The day is now the climax of weeks of festivities. Collectively the parades and costumes and balls are known as Carnival (in French, *carnival* means "to take away meat"). This time of celebration is so important in **Germany,** where it is called Fasching, that it is considered a fifth season.

On the first day of Carnival in **Switzerland**, everyone gets up just past midnight and heads for the center of town. At 4 a.m. all the lights of the city go out, and fifes and drums sound through the streets. Wearing masks and costumes, members of the Carnival guilds parade around. At dawn, everyone feasts on a Carnival breakfast of thick soup and cheese pastries.

In **Greece**, the final weeks before Lent are toasted with dance, drink, and feasting. Whitewashed streets vibrate with the color of Carnival costumes. (Keep in mind that because Greek Orthodox Churches don't celebrate Easter at the same time as Western churches, their Carnival is at a different time also. So most years you can attend two Carnival celebrations.)

In Patras, a port city on the Peloponnesian coast, Carnival is celebrated with a procession of chariots honoring the charioteer Pelops, mythical founder of the Olympic games. Another good place to spend Carnival in Greece is picturesque Naoussa, a fishing village on the island of Paros in Cyclades.

On the final Sunday before Lent, a special evening meal is held throughout Greece. Traditional dishes include macaroni, eggs, cheese pies, milk pie, and a dish called *tyrozoumi*, which is made of stewed wild herbs mixed with goat cheese. On the island of Karapathos, this meal takes place at the mayor's house.

On the island of Skyros, the last egg remaining from the meal is hung from the ceiling by a string. The guests, sitting around the table, hit at the egg with their foreheads to make it swing around, all the while trying to catch it with their lips. If an insect is seen crawling under the table after the meal, it is taken as a sign of prosperity. If someone sneezes during the meal, he will not live through the year. To prevent this evil fate, friends rip the sneezer's shirt open from throat to waist.

Carnival in **Venice** dates back to medieval times, when the city of canals gained recognition for its lavish masquerades and decorated gondolas.

St. Mark's Square is the center of Venice's modern-day Carnival festivities. Colorful masqueraders stroll through the piazza, stopping sometimes to pose for spectators. Performers present a series of short plays and operas from a specially built stage. These public performances are open to everyone. However, if you're also interested in seeing the private theater shows, you'll have to arrange tickets (not always an easy task).

The Venetians' favorite Carnival costumes are derived from characters in the Italian and French *Comedia dell' Arte*, a popular theater form in the 16th through 18th centuries. The *Comedia dell' Arte* was the sitcom of its day, with a continuing cast of characters that moved through comedic situations. Figures we know well, such as Harlequin, come from the *Comedia*.

In addition to the costumes from the Comedy of Art, Venetians also don a costume known as the *bauta*. It consists of a long black coat with a hood, a white or black mask, a frill covering the jaw, a black silk or lace mantle falling to the elbow, and a tricorn hat.

Belgium also salutes Carnival. In Malmedy, you can watch a torchlight parade. Aalst ends Carnival with an onion battle and a formal procession of *viuls Jeannettes* (dirty Jennies) wearing castoff clothing. At 4 a.m. on Shrove Tuesday in Binche, 30 miles south of Brussels, costumed townspeople are drummed out of their homes to dance through the streets all day long. Using oranges to symbolize the balls of Incan gold given to revelers during the 16th century by their king, the townspeople engage in a mock battle of the oranges.

Malaga hosts the most elaborate Carnival celebration along **Spain's** coast. It features parades, outdoor dances, costume competitions, and performances of satirical songs. Peninsular Spain's most flamboyant and best-known Carnival celebration is held in Cadiz. *Comparsas* and *chirigotas*, troupes of troubadours, roam the city's old quarter playing drums and blowing horns. During Cadiz's costume parade, hundreds of spectators accompany floats through town. And at midnight on the day of the Domingo de Pinatas, hollow papier mache dummies filled with toys are hung from trees and lampposts throughout the city. They are broken open and their contents distributed to the onlookers. Carnival ends with a display of fireworks along Cadiz's waterfront.

Late February: Ash Wednesday

Since the sixth century, this day has marked the beginning of Lent. In the Middle Ages, sinners came to church on this day dressed in sackcloth to be showered with ashes and thus absolved of their sins. Sackcloth and ashes remain symbols of penance, and Catholics still go to mass on this day to receive crosses of ashes on their foreheads.

Early March: Pero Palo Festival

One of **Spain's** oldest and strangest rituals is the Pero Palo festival in Villanueva de la Vera, a town 20 miles from Caceres. On the first night of the festival, the Pero Paleros (young men assigned to the task of creating and then destroying the Pero Palo dummy) take the remains of the last year's effigy, mend the suit, and fill the figure with straw. Their handiwork is accompanied by a dirge and the playing of drums.

The Pero Palo dummy, which represents the devil, is life-sized,

with a wooden head and a pointed black hat. He wears a black
suit, white gloves, and a spotted scarf around his shoulders. He
carries a cigar in his mouth. The dummy is impaled upon a
wooden pitchfork.

On the second day of the festival, Pero Palo is carried around
town on the shoulders of the townspeople. He is eventually taken
to the plaza, where he is passed through double rows of Pero
Paleros and shaken vigorously in a traditional dance.

On the third day, the dummy faces trial. The Pero Paleros
select a tribunal, then pin a notice on the dummy's back reading,
"Condemned to death for high treason by the Popular Tribunal."
By the end of the day, the effigy is decapitated. His body is placed
in a basket to the sounds of funeral drums.

Finally, the remains of Pero Palo are thrown into the air. He is
beaten by the townspeople until no straw remains inside him.
Then he's carried away in a wheelbarrow and buried to the sound
of drum rolls. The wild party that ends the festivities is said to
keep the town's birthrate high.

The origin of the Pero Palo trial is unclear. The name Pero is a
diminutive of Pedro, the name used in many Spanish festivals for
the scapegoat effigy.

Mid-March: Fallas of St. Joseph

This day in honor of St. Joseph, the earthly father of Jesus,
dates back to medieval times, when carpenters swept out shavings
that had collected in their shops during the year and burned them
in a bonfire.

In **Valencia, Spain**, the celebration of the feast day lasts an
entire week. For the event, the townspoeple build *fallas*, gigantic
constructions of wood and papier mache, which represent
mythical monsters and people and satirical scenes on a gargantuan
scale. The *fallas* mock everything from religion to taxes. Each is
sponsored by a neighborhood or association and built in secret.
The *fallas*, which can cost millions of dollars to build, are
launched at once onto the streets of Valencia. Following the

festivities, all but the chosen few *fallas* are burned.

March: Holy Week

Holy Week (the week before Easter Sunday) begins with Palm Sunday, commemorating Christ's arrival in Jerusalem. He was greeted with palm branches, which the townspeople laid at his feet. If you visit St. Peter's Square in **Rome** on Palm Sunday, you can see the pope being carried in his chair through the square amid dazzling pageantry as he blesses the palms for distribution.

In **Austria**, farmers make *Palmbuschen* on Palm Sunday, mounting holly leaves, willow boughs, and cedar twigs atop tree-size poles. The farmers have the *Palmbuschen* blessed and keep them to ward off storms and sickness during the coming year.

In **Spain**, Holy Week resurrects the mystical religious world of medieval times. Candlelight processions mourning the death of Christ file silently through the old quarters of Spain's cities and towns. Statues depicting the life of Christ are carried through the streets. In some areas, residents don the attire of Biblical times and re-enact the life of Jesus.

If you visit the old quarter of Cuenca, Spain during Holy Week, you can watch a procession of silent penitents bearing sculpted scenes from the Passion. Religious Music Week is also held in Cuenca at this time. Well-known musicians perform at San Miguel Church.

In Malaga, magnificent statues are carried before the public on baroque thrones by "throne men." Statues of the Virgin are dressed with sumptuous shawls embroidered in silver and gold. Malaga's procession of Our Lady of Sorrows is especially beautiful as it winds its way through the streets, lit by penitents' candles.

The celebration of Holy Week in Seville is elaborate. More than 50 orders of priests march in procession following an ancient route from the Plaza de la Campana along picturesque Sierpes Street, past the town hall, and through the Gothic cathedral. They end up in front of the Giralda (the landmark tower built during the

Moorish occupation of Spain) and the baroque Bishop's Palace.
The procession includes more than 40 *pasos* (platforms of wood
and silver), which represent scenes from the Passion. They are
covered with carnations and rock gently on the shoulders of the
bearers to the rhythm of the *saetas*, short and fervent prayers.

Processions continue throughout the week in Valladolid, Spain.
The most important events here take place on Good Friday. At
noon an open-air sermon is given in the Plaza Mayor just before
the start of a religious procession, which includes 29 monumental
pasos.

In Jumilla, Murcia province, a procession depicting Jesus'
entry into Jerusalem opens the Holy Week celebrations. Costumed
residents play the roles of Jesus and the apostles. A nighttime
penitential procession on Holy Tuesday leads through the old
quarter. The only light comes from bonfires and the candles
carried by the members of different lay brotherhoods. The
procession in honor of Jesus being arrested takes place on
Wednesday. The most solemn procession, the burial of Christ, is
held Good Friday evening. The climax is a procession on Sunday
morning, the Procession of the Resurrection.

In **Salzburg**, the week before Christ's resurrection is celebrated with a music festival that includes operas and symphonic
and choral concerts.

The celebration of Holy Week in **Oberammergau, Germany**
is elaborate—even if it does take place only once every 10 years.
The inhabitants of this remote village in the shadow of the
Bavarian Alps stage a play depicting the Passion of Christ.
Everyone in the town participates in some way, and preparations
for the event begin a year in advance.

The performance of the Oberammergau Passion Play dates
back to 1634, when it was staged in thanksgiving for the end of
the Black Plague. The townspeople pledged then that their descen-
dants would continue performing the play every 10 years until the
end of time. Wars and economic problems in Germany sometimes
have affected the time of the performance, but the tradition has

continued. The next Passion Play is planned for 1990.

March 15: Reindeer-Driving Competitions

Reindeer are essential to the survival of the Lapps in **Finland**.
But in recent years, reindeer-driving has become a sport as well as
a means of survival. The annual roundups are held at Inari. During
the most impressive, men and women on cross-country skis
compete to be the fastest to herd 100 reindeer over a 3 1/4-mile
course.

March 17: St. Patrick's Day

This, the day of St. Patrick's death, is one of the most
important holidays in **Ireland**, and it is celebrated with great
religious devotion. Unlike people in the United States, the Irish
consider St. Patrick's Day much more than an excuse for a party.

Born in Britain in A.D. 385, Magnus Sucatus Patricus was
taken captive at age 16 by Irish raiders plundering along the coast
of England. For six years, he was forced to herd sheep in the Irish
countryside. When he finally escaped, Patrick returned to Britain
and entered a monastery to become a monk. But he couldn't
forget the Irish, who were under the domination of pagan Druids.
So he began his journey back to Ireland, founding hundreds of
churches and schools and converting people to Christianity along
the way.

Patrick explained the Trinity using the three-leaved shamrock
as an analogy. Thus, on St. Patrick's Day the Irish dress in green
and display the shamrock. (They're also known to enjoy a pint or
two of ale in remembrance of their saint.)

Late March: Easter Sunday

For Christians, Easter Sunday is the most important day of the
year. It is a lunar holiday that takes place on the first Sunday
following the full moon that appears on or after the vernal
equinox. Although today the holiday celebrates Christ's resurrec-

tion, Easter originally was a pagan springtime festival. Many of the traditions surrounding the day have nothing to do with Christianity.

According to scripture, Mary Magdalen and some companions went early this morning to the cave where Jesus had been buried on Good Friday. They found the cave empty. An Angel of the Lord appeared, explaining that Jesus had risen from the dead. Because of this (and also because, according to legend, the sun dances for joy as it rises on this monring), many sunrise services are conducted on Easter Day.

Following the religious ceremony, many Europeans enjoy the tradition of taking an Easter walk through the countryside, showing off their new Easter outfits (wearing a piece of new clothing on Easter is supposed to bring luck for the rest of the year).

Easter is also the day the Easter rabbit brings decorated hard-boiled eggs to English children. (In the eighth century, the Venerable Bede suggested that the word *Easter* probably came from *Eostre*, the Anglo-Saxon name of a Teutonic goddess of spring and fertility. Eostre's symbol was the hare.)

The egg has become a special Easter symbol of rebirth, perhaps because eggs were one of the foods forbidden during Lent. The custom of dyeing eggs comes to us from medieval Egyptians and Persians, who colored eggs for their spring celebrations.

In **Greece** the day of Christ's resurrection (which may not fall on the same day as our Easter) is the most important public holiday. It is marked by meals of spit-roasted lamb, pastries, and hard-boiled eggs dyed red. The feasts are followed by folk dancing in regional costumes. Easter fairs are held at Tripolis, Trapeza, and Livadia, where roast lamb and delicious local wines are offered to visitors.

April.1: April Fool's Day

April Fool's Day began because New Year's Day occurred during Easter week. Until the 16th century, the new year began at the time of the Vernal Equinox—which is also when Easter occurs each year. The people celebrated the new year with an eight-day festival that ended April 1, when they exchanged gifts. Churchmen didn't like the New Year's festivities outshadowing Easter Day, and they wanted to change New Year's to another day.

However, even after most European countries had accepted the Gregorian calendar, which changed the celebration of New Year's Day from April 1 to January 1, many refused to give up the old customs and continued to celebrate the new year on April 1. They were mocked as April fools. The tradition of making fun of April fools eventually evolved into a custom of making fun of anyone at all on this day.

In **France**, the April fool is called the *poisson d'avril*. Children try to pin a paper *poisson* (fish) on peoples' backs without getting caught. And pastry makers will sell you a bun in the shape of a fish.

April: Spring Carnival

The week following Easter is a passionate Carnival time in **Seville**—perhaps the most colorful festival time in all Europe. During this week, Sevilians break loose after the severity and fasting of Lent and Holy Week. Their annual fair is famous for two things: bullfights and flamenco dancing.

During the fair, the streets smell of orange blossoms, carnations, and geraniums. In the afternoons, people dress up to take horse-drawn carriages to the bullfights, which last until about 8 p.m. Then they make their way home for a nap before dinner, which is served at midnight. After dinner, it's time to watch the flamenco dancing by the gypsies, which continues until dawn. The fairgrounds are lined with small wooden shacks called *casetas*, where the dancers perform.

April: Festivals of Spring

Each spring, herdsmen all over Europe lead their goats and cattle up into the mountain pastures for summer grazing. The **Swiss**, who see this ascent into the mountains as the true beginning of spring, dress in traditional costumes for the trek. And they decorate their prize cows with flowers.

Even though the people in **Zurich** don't have any cows to decorate, they celebrate the beginning of spring as well, with the **Six O'Clock Ringing**. On the first day of this festival, children parade through the streets of the city. On the second day, members of Zurich's historic craft guilds dress in medieval costume and follow the route of the children. At 6 p.m. everyone gathers in the town square to listen to the church bells ringing and to watch the burning of Boegg, a white figure symbolizing winter.

In **Holland**, spring is welcomed with the annual Tulip Festival. At the world's largest flower garden in Keukenhof, near Lisse, you can see 70 acres of tulips, dahlias, daffodils, hyacinths, and other spring blooms from late March through May.

Mid-April: Festival of the Sardine

This nighttime tradition in **Murcia, Spain** marks the end of the Easter season—and is probably the origin of the college panty raid! Men carrying torches escort a parade that includes 25 carriages, each with an accompanying group of merrymakers, bands, and *hachoneros*, or men who carry bras. Little toys are thrown to the spectators from the carriages.

The parade continues to the old bridge in Puente Viejo. Here, at midnight, the paraders burn a huge papier-mache *sardina* (sardine), and fireworks are set off.

The Burial of the Sardine dates back to the 19th century, when university students, who could afford to eat nothing but sardines, would bury some when they graduated.

Late April: Feast of St. George

St. George was **England's** most celebrated knight on a white charger. He rode into Cappadocia wearing shining armor to slay the dragon and save the princess. During the Crusades, King Richard the Lionhearted was heard to call on "St. George for England."

In the village of Kalliopi on the **Greek** island of Limnos, St. George's day is celebrated with horse races. A three-day feast marks the occasion in Arahova. And in Assi Gonia near Hania on the Greek island of Crete, the feast is followed by a sheep-shearing competition among the local shepherds. In the village of Pili on the island of Cos, a day of horse racing is followed by an evening of dancing.

The biggest and perhaps the best re-enactment of the battles between the Moors and the Christians takes place in **Alicante, Spain** and coincides with the Feast of St. George. A castle stage set, sumptuous costumes, musket fire, and battle regalia make this festival worth seeing.

April 30: Walpurgis Eve

In **Uppsala**, Sweden's major university town, Walpurgis Eve is a time when alumni and students wear white caps and gather to celebrate the rebirth of spring and the death of winter. They march in a torchlight parade and celebrate until dawn. Thousands join in the hymns to spring and listen to the speeches about the end of winter.

This night, according to legend, is also a time when witches ride. It is the night before the birthday of St. Walpurgis, the medieval protectress against magic. In the Middle Ages, people knew that the witches were out on this night and wanted to prevent them from casting evil spells. So they rang church bells, clattered pots and pans, and carried torches topped with hemlock, rosemary, and juniper. In **Austria**, people still stick brooms and rakes into the ground upside down, hoping to snag the witches as they ride by.

May 1: May Day

Originally, May Day was set aside for the worship of tree spirits, who the people believed gave rain and sunshine and made crops grow. Even today, **Swedish** peasants place leafy branches in their cornfields on this day to ensure a good crop. And in **Germany** and **France**, the farmers decorate a large branch or an entire tree with stalks of grain and bring it home with them on the last wagon leaving the harvest field.

Flowers are also an important part of the May Day celebration. The Romans began this tradition by offering flowers to Flora, their goddess of spring, on May 1 each year.

Modern maidens no longer rise at dawn on May Day to gather flowers and tree branches, but in many town squares throughout Europe you still can see maypoles decorated with colorful streamers.

May: The Brighton Festival

The seaside town of **Brighton, England**, which combines Regency elegance with a vivid history, is the perfect setting for England's largest festival. The Brighton Festival features a program of classical concerts, opera, theater, cabaret, dance, film, literary events, exhibitions, rock music, pop music, children's entertainment, and community events.

Second Sunday in May: Cat Procession

In the Middle Ages, the people of **Belgium** believed that cats held great powers. In A.D. 962, Baudowin III, count of Flanders, decided to put an end to all the superstitions. He threw a couple live cats out the window of his castle—and lived to tell about it. From time to time, the people decided to re-enact Count Baudowin's courageous act (just to reassure themselves). They continued the tradition until 1817, when it was decided that toy cats should be used instead of live ones.

Today, Belgians celebrate the day by dressing as cats and

marching in the Cat Parade at Ypres. Feline floats carry Puss-in-Boots, Cieper (the king of the cats), his wife Minneke Poes, and their kitten Pieperte.

Mid-May through the third week in June: Vienna International Festival

During this festival celebrating the best of the world's musicians, operas are staged at the State Opera House, symphonic and choral concerts and chamber music recitals take place at the Konzerthaus, and sacred music is played at the Church of the Augustinian Friars.

Mid- to late May: Well-Dressing

For centuries the people of **England** worshipped their wells. They believed powerful spirits lived in them and provided the water. They took great care to decorate (or dress) their wells with flowers. Eventually the dressing became more elaborate, as the people pressed flower petals, leaves, bark, moss, and cones into clay, creating pictures.

Today, the British take their well-dressing very seriously. Tissington is the oldest and most famous home of well-dressing, and people come from all over the world to see the festivities here each year. Work continues late into the night in Tissington on the days of well-dressing. Farmers, typists, and housewives volunteer to prepare the elaborate pictures that on Ascension Day (May 28) adorn the five wells of the village.

Late May: The Bath Festival

Bath, England's graceful Georgian architecture is a fitting backdrop for one of Europe's most prestigious international festivals. During the Bath Festival, the city is filled with more than 1,000 performers who sing choral works by composers such as Gluck, Monteverdi, and Purcell. Other events include opera performances, orchestral and chamber music, jazz, a contemporary art fair, marionette shows, a walking tour, film shows, art exhibitions, and garden tours. There is even an off-Broadway festival in Bath with fringe performances.

Late May: Glyndebourne Music Festival

This annual celebration of music near London, **England** focuses primarily on opera. For information or tickets to this internationally respected festival, contact the Glyndebourne Opera Festival Box Office.

June 1: Procession des Bouteilles

If you're in **Boulbon** in the south of France on this day, don't be surprised to see men walking through the streets carrying bottles of wine. Even the town officials and clergymen join in the parade in celebration of the region's new wine. If you follow the parade, you won't end up in the town pub, but in the 12th-century Chapel of St. Marcellin. When the sermon is finished, all the men uncork their wine bottles and swallow in unison.

June 6: Corpus Christi

In **Spain**, this celebration of the Eucharist is a joyous holiday. Townspeople parade through the streets, which are carpeted with flower petals strewn by children wearing First Communion garb. In Toledo, where the feast was first celebrated in 1280, the procession is preceded by dancers covered with ribbons. Behind the dancers comes a parade of silver crosses and a gold 16th-century cross, carried by priests and members of various brotherhoods dressed in red or white tunics. In Redondela, the people perform a sword dance around the Host.

Mid-June: The Royal Ascot

The annual horse race known as the Royal Ascot is a splendid **English** tradition begun by Queen Anne in 1711. She encouraged horse breeding and racing by establishing prizes, or Royal Plates as they became known. On her death, Ascot meetings became less regal, until 1825 when George IV began the Royal Procession and gave the races the character they possess today.

The Royal Family attends Ascot, pulling up to its place in the Royal Enclosure in horse-drawn carriages. If you are lucky enough to be invited to watch the races from the Royal Enclosure, remember to dress the part. Morning coats and top hats are de rigueur for men. Women wear dresses, wide-brimmed flowery hats, and gloves.

The Ascot is perhaps more a social occasion than a horse race. Business groups and social clubs usually arrange tents, where, if you are invited, you can spend hours eating, drinking, and chatting. If you are not invited to attend one of the catered affairs, bring a picnic lunch to enjoy on the grass surrounding the track.

Mid-June: Midsummer Day

Delarna Province in the heart of **Sweden** has preserved the pagan rites of Midsummer (with a Christian touch these days). Swedes begin the day by going to church—they get there aboard locally made rowboats adorned with greenery. Throughout the day, children race through the forests gathering birch boughs and wildflowers to decorate the town square. A pole (similar to a maypole) is raised, and villagers dance around it through the night (actually, the sun sets for only a few minutes), weaving the long ribbons that hang from the top.

Young girls are said to dream of their beloved on Midsummer Night if they place a bouquet containing seven wildflowers under their pillows. And if they look into a reflecting pool on Midsummer Day, the next man they see will be their loved one. On Midsummer Morning, the dew supposedly cures all ills.

The most colorful Midsummer celebrations in Sweden are in the villages around Lake Siljan: Rattvik, Leksand, and Tallberg.

Bonfires (known as Midsummer fires) play an important part in Midsummer celebrations throughout Europe. In **Denmark**, thousands of bonfires are lit along the coast, and the people row out to sea to watch the reflections. And in **Norway**, farmers believe their crops will grow as high as they can jump over the fires.

June 24: The Fiesta of San Juan

The Feast of St. Juan, which coincides with the vernal equinox, is a time of Midsummer revelry. In towns throughout **Spain**, the people picnic or spend the day at the beach. In Alicante, bonfires are set off. In Malaga, an effigy of San Juan is burned. In Soria, volunteers walk barefoot on a bed of hot coals. And in Menorca, the festivals include a figure dressed in animal skins representing the saint, acrobatics on horses, and medieval games.

Early July: Shrimp Festival

Belgium celebrates its shrimp industry with this Midsummer festival. For centuries, Belgian fishermen have ridden their horses into the North Sea, dragging nets. When their nets were filled with shrimp, the men returned to shore to transfer the shrimp to the baskets hanging from the horses' flanks.

Oostduinkerke is the only town where you still can watch this picturesque custom of shrimping on horseback. After the shrimp are brought to shore, you can sample them, freshly boiled. The day's shrimping is followed by a ball and a parade by the sea.

Early July: La Tour de France

Every year at the beginning of July a shot rings out in **Paris**, triggering the start of the annual Tour de France bicycle race. Participants pedal over more than 2,500 miles (4,000 kilometers) of roadway in a clockwise circle around the country. The race dates back to 1903, when Henri Desgrange, editor of a daily sports publication, came up with the idea of a bicycle race that circled France.

In the flatlands of Normandy and Brittany, cyclists can cover as much as 160 miles per day. The distance gained here helps compensate for the slow going through the Alps and the Pyrenees.

Participants race in teams of 10, riding each day for three weeks, with one day of rest. The race concludes on the Champs-Elysees in Paris.

July 2 and August 16: The Palio of the Contrade

The Palio, one of the most genuine and fascinating of all **Italian** spectacles, is a bareback three-lap horse race around the shell-shaped Piazza del Campo in Siena. It lasts all of 90 seconds but generates feuds that continue for decades. Run twice a summer, the Palio is a competition between 10 of Siena's 17 *contrade*, or districts. During the days preceding the race, the people of Siena revert to the venality of the Middle Ages. Bribery, meddling, and skulduggery are not only permitted but also encouraged. *Contrade* captains are *expected* to indulge in intrigue as part of their efforts to outdo their rivals. Millions of lire are spent bribing the jockeys.

On the day of the race, flag twirlers, trumpeters, guards armed with ancient crossbows, drummer boys, horsemen in armor, and horses in leather and brass strut up and down Siena's winding streets. Thousands of spectators crowd around the dirt track bordering the Piazza del Campo.

At 5 p.m. the start of the official Palio parade is signaled with cannon fire. Church bells toll. Each of the 17 *contrade* displays its distinguishing color. Young men in tights and tunics throw their flags into the air, catching them with precision. Brigades move down the streets. Onlookers have been known to faint from all the excitement.

At about 7 p.m. the horses trot onto the track. Their jockeys race them mercilessly around the track, whipping them all the while. The winner is carried shoulder high from the palazzo. The rest of the night is spent feasting and celebrating.

The Palio has its roots in the Middle Ages, when Siena was an independent republic. At that time, the 17 *contrade* were separate military societies, each defended by its own military forces. Life in Siena in the Middle Ages was not easy. Homes were small, cold, badly ventilated, and had little light. The streets were narrow, murky, and bristled with potential ambush. The walls that surrounded the city and those of the high buildings along the streets were blackened by smoke. The danger of epidemic was great, as was the possibility of dying by the sword or dagger. Considering all this, it is no wonder the people looked for escape. The Compagnie Popolari were organized to help provide distraction. These companies, each from a different section of the city, were intended to keep the people happy and free from worries (and thoughts of revolt, no doubt) by initiating games, parties, balls, festivals, and plays. One of the games the Compagnie Popolari initiated was the Palio.

First Thursday in July: Brussels' Ommegang

In the Middle Ages, people marched around their towns to give them a magical protection. This tradition of the Ommegang (*om* means *around* and *gang* means *march* or *walk*) continues in **Brussels**.

Brussels' Ommegang has been an annual tradition since 1900. It imitates an Ommegang procession that took place in 1549, when ornately dressed Belgians paid their respects to the visiting Spanish Emperor Charles V and his family. They carried huge banners, wore the fancy dress of their royal families, held folk dances, and set off fireworks.

Today, this historic procession is held in the Grand' Place and celebrates the arrival of the statue of the Virgin Mary in the Sablon Church. The oldest and noblest families of the city take part in the procession.

July 7-15: The Running of the Bulls in Pamplona

This may be the world's ultimate display of *machismo*. The men of **Pamplona, Spain** pit their lives against hundreds of bulls set loose in the streets and herded toward the bull ring. The men dress in white pants and white shirts and tie red sashes around their waists and red scarves around their necks. Then, to display their courage, they run before the bulls, often injuring or killing themselves.

Festivities begin when a rocket is fired from the town hall. Then bands of bagpipers march through town announcing that the bulls are coming. Young people roam the streets singing, dancing, and drinking.

All this revelry is in the name of the town's patron saint, San Fermin, a bishop and martyr from Pamplona. Buried in Amiens, France, his body mysteriously disappeared. The body was miraculously found six centuries later, and, according to legend, although it was midwinter, the trees burst into leaf.

In addition to the famous running of the bulls, this fiesta features a parade, folk dancing, fireworks, and a week-long, nonstop party.

July 14: Bastille Day

In 1789, crowds of **Parisians** stormed the Bastille prison. To them, this stronghold symbolized the oppression of the ruling monarchy. The mobs freed the prisoners and tore down the prison, stone by stone. This act of rebellion marked the beginning of the French Revolution. Today, Bastille Day is a national holiday throughout France, celebrated with fireworks and parades. Many Paris fire stations sponsor dinners and balls the night before, with brass bands, a buffet with wine, and dancing. It's a great occasion—you can spend an evening mingling with the French for about $6.

July 22: Anniversary of the Pied Piper of Hamelin

A stranger came into **Hamelin, Germany** in the 14th century and struck a deal with the townspeople. Hamelin was having problems with rats—lots of rats. The stranger promised to get ride of all the rats, and the townspeople promised to pay him in return. The stranger played his pipe, and all the rats followed him out of town and into the river. Although the piper had kept his part of the bargain, the townspeople refused to pay him. He left town and returned later wearing a disguise. He played his pipe again. This time, all the children of the town followed him to the river. They never returned. Hamelin remembers the legend of the Pied Piper by re-enacting the story at noon one Sunday each summer.

Late July: World Soccer Cup

Soccer teams from more than 100 countries compete every four years for the World Cup. The teams compete for six to eight months prior to the tournament to decide which ones will be able to participate. Twenty-four finalist teams travel to the host country to play in the 50 games of the event. (The first international soccer match was held in 1904. Belgium and France competed for the title.)

Late July to late August: Salzburg Festival

Perhaps the most important and most well-known of all the **Austrian** music festivals, the Salzburg Festival has been an annual event since 1920. It features opera, symphonic concerts, ecclesiastical opera, choral music, chamber music, instrumental and lieder recitals, ballet performances, and sacred music.

Tickets to this king of European festivals are very expensive. Nonetheless, requests for tickets each year outnumber available places by about four to one. And hotel accommodations for the days of the event are scarcer still.

But anyone who has been to the Salzburg Festival can tell you that it's worth all the trouble and the expense. The performers are the best in the world, the audiences are distinguished and reverent, and you can't help but feel you're hearing Mozart for the first time.

July to August: Wine Festivals

As home to Dionysius, the god of wine, **Greece** hosts annual wine festivals known for their revelry, dancing, and singing. You can enjoy complimentary glasses of wine and join in the folk dancing. Good places to sample the regional Greek wines are Daphni (10 kilometers from Athens), Alexandroupoulos (in Northern Greece), and Rethymnon and Heraklion (in Crete).

Late July to August: Bayreath Music Festival

This month-long celebration in **Germany** is devoted exclusively to the music of Wagner. National music groups perform the works. If you're interested in attending, send away for tickets at least a year in advance—this is a well-known and popular celebration.

Early August: Eisteddfod

Eisteddfod is a literary competition intended to help **Wales** celebrate and remember Welsh, one of Europe's oldest written languages. Only those who can write in Welsh can participate. The winners of the competition are chosen by the Gorsedd, the national bardic assembly. One contestant is named bard of the year. He leads the procession of winners, all dressed in Druidic robes, to the central pavilion in Wales.

Early August: The Edinburgh International Festival

Edinburgh, England has sponsored its annual international arts festival since 1946. Today the event is respected as the most comprehensive festival of its kind in the world. About a half-million visitors turn out each year to enjoy the exhibitions, opera, theater, and dance performances. You can take in everything from the Scottish Chamber Orchestra playing in the 18th century Hopetoun House to rock multimedia happenings on the steps of the post office.

While the Edinburgh Festival is known primarily as a music and theater festival, it is also a stage for some of the best avant-garde productions in the English language. The Fringe, as this part of the festival is known, boasts more than 9,000 innovative and low-budget productions. The Fringe is much more freewheeling than the main festival, because anyone is permitted to perform.

The open nature of the Fringe is both good and bad. It allows creative people a chance to show what they can do. But it also makes for an uneven quality of performances, which include theater, comedy, musicals, cabaret, opera, mime, children's shows, folk music, jazz, rock music, and poetry readings.

Considering the multitude of offerings, the problem is to separate the wheat from the chaff. One of the best ways to do this is to hang out at the Edinburgh bars that are popular among the avant-garde theater crowd, including the Assembly Room, the Fringe Club, the Theater Workshop Bar, and the Travers Theater Bar. You can find out a lot about companies and performers over a pint of ale.

Last Saturday in August: Giants Festival

All the participants in this festival are larger than life (literally). Held annually in **Ath**, 30 miles southeast of Brussels, the Giants Festival re-enacts the wedding ceremony of Goliath and his bride (two huge wicker-frame giants). Following the ceremony, the bridegroom battles David in a play that dates back to the Middle Ages. The next day, the victorious Goliath and his bride lead a parade through town.

Late August to early September: Schueberfo'er

Luxembourg's country fair dates back to 1340, when John the Blink, count of Luxembourg and king of Bohemia, decided to organize a get-together for the country's shepherds. Today, the shepherds dress in costume and lead their sheep, decorated with colored ribbons, through the Place du Glacis as a band plays *Hammelsmarch* (Sheep's March). You can walk along the midway, playing the games and enjoying the folklore displays, or pause for a stein of beer at one of the beer tents.

Early September: Braemar Highland Gathering

Everyone participating in this **Scottish** festival must don traditional kilts for the occasion. The annual gathering dates back to the 11th century, when King Malcolm called his clans together at Braemar. He wanted to choose the strongest soldiers and the quickest messengers to serve him, so he had all the clansmen compete in tests of strength and speed. Today, as in the days of King Malcolm, Scottsmen toss the caber (a pole 16 to 20 feet long weighing 120 pounds) so that it lands on its opposite end. (Loggers once threw logs across rivers in this manner.)

September: Harvest Festivals

After a summer of working in the fields and bringing in the crops, Europeans are ready to have a good time. In southern **Spain**, farmers and winemakers celebrate the grape harvest. The sherry Vintage Fiesta takes place in Jerez de la Frontera. After a thanksgiving service, the townspeople turn out for the parade. Horsemen in Spanish costume ride through the streets. The parade is followed by horse races and bullfights.

In Zaragoza, the harvest festival coincides with the Holy Cross celebrations and features grape stomping in the town's main plaza. At the Ciudad Real Festival, you can sample typical Manchegan food, as well as the famous local wines.

Perhaps the most important Spanish grape harvest festival takes place in Cadiz, known for its sherry. You can watch the blessing of the harvested grapes and the new wine, as well as parades and flamenco competitions.

The Swiss city of **Bern** celebrates the harvest season with an onion market. In the 15th century, the town of Fribourg sent men to help rebuild Bern after it was nearly destroyed by a fire. To show their gratitude, the people of Bern allowed Fribourg to sell its onions at Bern markets. Today, Bern's onion market is well-known. The market square overflows with onions, onion soup, onion-stuffed sausages, onion salad, and even onion cake.

Mid-September: Oktoberfest

In 1810 the 40,000 royal merrymakers at Prince Ludwig's

wedding reception began a tradition that has become **Germany's** most famous beer festival: Oktoberfest.

Oktoberfest begins three Saturdays before the first Sunday in October and continues for 16 days. The festivities begin with a parade through the streets of Munich to the Theresienwiese (a meadow named after Prince Ludwig's bride). Here, after horse-drawn beer wagons arrive, the mayor taps the first of more than 700,000 kegs. Thousands of revelers quaff specially brewed Octoberfest beer and enjoy oompah music.

Enormous beer tents, sponsored by Germany's 13 major breweries, are the hub of activity. Stein-serving waitresses weave among wooden tables. Outside the tents, midway rides and sideshows contribute to the carnival atmosphere.

On the second day of Oktoberfest, from 10:30 a.m. until noon, a folklore parade features groups in national costume from all parts of Germany. After this, it's back to the beer gardens, which remain open from noon until 10:30 p.m. Spend the afternoon drinking and feasting on *weisswuerste* (white sausage). By nightfall, you'll be ready to join in the rousing, if slightly slurred, renditions of *In Munchen steht ein Hofbraeuhaus.*

Mid-October: International Marathon

This international marathon attracts thousands of athletes to **Greece** each year. Participants in the race retrace Pheidippidis' route from Marathon to Athens to announce the Athenian victory over the invading Persians in 490 B.C. The course of the race covers 26 miles, and the finish line is at Athens Olympic Stadium. Participation in the event is open to everyone.

Mid-October: Exaltation of the Shellfish

Each year **Pontevedra,** in the northwest part of **Spain,** sponsors a huge exposition, competition, and market, all in honor of the region's major industry: shellfishing. The day begins with mass. Afterward, the townspeople dress in traditional costume and perform Galician dances called *muneiras*. After the day of celebrating, the town gathers for a typical Galician meal, featuring shrimp, lobsters, and mussels.

October 31: Halloween

The **Irish** have celebrated Samhain, the beginning of the Celtic year, every Nov. 1 since the third century B.C. This ancient harvest festival honored the lord of the dead. Today the celebrating continues. Only now Samhain is known as Halloween.

Literally, Samhain means "the end of summer." Originally, the festival not only marked the end of one year and the beginning of another, but also a turning point in the grazing cycle, when the flocks were brought in from their summer pastures. The herdsmen returned for the winter, and the clan gathered to welcome them home with feasts and bonfires.

Despite the festivities, however, Samhain was also a solemn occasion. The growing season had ended, and it was time to prepare for winter. In a sense, Samhain was a celebration of death, and the Celts used it as a time to honor their ancestors.

The Celts believed that on Samhain the spirits of all the people who had died during the previous year gathered together and had to be led out of town. The Celts also believed that on this day the barriers between the supernatural world and the mortal world were suspended. Ghosts, demons, and the *sidh* (deities now known as fairies) were visible and mingled freely among men. During this time, the entrances to the spirit world stood open, and anyone brave enough could pass through. The people had their fortunes told, and sacrifices (possibly human) were made.

In the ninth century, the Catholic Church made November 1 All Saints' (or All Hallows') Day. The festival of Samhain was so popular that the Church wisely decided not to do away with it, despite its pagan origins. Instead, Samhain was made a Church holiday, and Oct. 31 became All Hallows' Eve (Halloween).

For centuries, the two traditions have peacefully coexisted. All Saints' Day remains a holy day of obligation for Catholics around the world. But the pagan rituals of Samhain Eve rule the day before.

Seasonal foods, especially apples, are an important part of Halloween, as they were important to Samhain. The best-known Halloween dish is *bairin breac*. Hidden inside this fruit cake are objects that foretell the future of the person who finds them. A ring means marriage; a coin, wealth; a thimble, spinsterhood.

The jack-o'-lantern, according to Irish legend, descends from a fellow named Jack, who was too greedy to get into heaven and on bad terms with the devil, so he couldn't get into hell. The devil threw Jack a lighted coal to taunt him, and Jack stuck it in the turnip he was eating. Jack wanders still, searching for a final resting place, his path lighted by his turnip.

November 5: Guy Fawkes' Day

Guy Fawkes and his group of conspirators planned in 1605 to blow up King James I and his government. However, King James' scouts got wind of the impending disaster and managed to confiscate the 36 barrels of gunpowder that Guy Fawkes' men had hidden beneath **England's** Houses of Parliament. Parliament was so relieved that it declared a national holiday on the anniversary of the discovery of the plot. The British remember the day with effigies of Guy Fawkes, which are carried through town by children, then burned in a bonfire.

Guy Fawkes' Eve (November 4) has become the traditional night for mischief throughout England (kind of Great Britain's answer to Halloween). English children enjoy this, their "lawless night," and spend it setting off firecrackers, taking garden gates off their hinges, and otherwise annoying their elders.

December: Christmas Markets

During the first three weeks of December, Europeans make it easy for you to do your Christmas shopping. Special holiday markets are set up throughout **Germany** and **Austria**.

Munich is the site of Germany's oldest Christmas market—it

was begun more than 600 years ago. The stalls are set up each year on the Marienplatz, near the 15th-century old town hall. You'll find lots of seasonal goodies, including intricately hand-crafted toys and tree ornaments and ornately carved Christmas figurines. But even if you're not in the mood for shopping, you can walk through the fair and enjoy the creches, the Christmas trees, and the holiday music. Or enjoy a *lebkuchen,* a special Christmas cookie full of spices.

Perhaps the most well-known of Europe's Christmas markets is the one in **Nuremburg**, the toy capital of Germany. This fair, which dates back to 1639, is the largest in Germany and lasts three weeks. A girl dressed as the Christ Child steps onto the balcony of the town church and announces that the fair is open. At the Nuremburg market, you'll find handmade ornaments, holiday candles, embroidery, wreaths, creches, and, of course, lots of edibles, including *lebkucken* and gingerbread houses (Nuremburg gingerbread bakers are world-famous).

Music is an important part of the **Frankfurt** Christmas market, which begins each year during the last weekend in November. Every Wednesday and Saturday during this fair, trumpet musicians play Christmas and Advent carols. Also on Saturdays, the Glockenspiel from the Nicolaus Church is played. On Christmas Eve, the 9 churches in downtown Frankfurt sound their bells simultaneously for 30 minutes.

In **Marseilles, France**, you can visit the Santon Fair throughout December. A *santon* is a small clay and straw figure representing something from Biblical times (although modern figures are made, too). Local families create the *santons,* following models that have been passed on from generation to generation since the 17th century.

One of **Rome's** most colorful Christmas festivities is the wholesale market held each December 23 at Via Ostiense. Going from stall to stall at this fair, you can find Italian holiday delicacies at wholesale prices. This all-night buying spree, locally known as *il cottio*, is officially opened at 2 a.m., when the mayor arrives.

December: The Christmas Season

Christmas Day is one of the most joyous and important days of the Christian year. Christmas celebrates the birth of Jesus, the Messiah. The exact date of Jesus' birth has never been established. Nonetheless, in the fourth century, the church introduced a feast day at this time of year that has become accepted as Christ's birthday.

The church anniversary coincided with seasonal, non-Christian customs that have become part of the day's festivities. Burning the yule log, for example, was a pre-Christian custom that celebrated the return of the sun in the middle of winter. The evergreen, holly, and mistletoe are pre-Christian defiances against winter's barrenness. And the tradition of exchanging gifts began in the 12th century, inspired by the scriptural account of the Wise Men who brought gold, incense, and myrrh to the Christ Child.

However, Christmas is more than a day—it's a season. From the feast of the Immaculate Conception (December 8) through Epiphany (January 6), this time of year seems a continuous celebration. Throughout Europe, the streets are decorated with twinkling lights and alive with the singing of Christmas carols. In every church a creche scene is constructed, in every town square a tree is decorated, and in every home the family prepares for the feasting and gift-giving of Christmas Day.

The creche (or crib) is a display showing Jesus in the humble surroundings of his birth. He is surrounded by oxen and donkeys. St. Francis was the first to come up with the idea of the creche scene. He wrote to a friend that he wanted to create a special outdoor Christmas display.

The Protestant reformer Martin Luther is responsible for the link between the fir tree and the Christmas season. While returning home one Christmas Eve through the snow, he looked up to see the stars glittering above a forest of fir trees. He wanted his family to see what he had seen, so he chopped down one of the trees and took it home with him. He covered the tree with tiny lighted candles to represent the stars.

During the weeks preceding Christmas, mummers (actors dressed in costumes to conceal their identities) perform plays throughout **England**. It's a tradition that dates back to the 14th century. An actor dressed as Father Christmas usually opens the proceedings. Then St. George takes on his enemies, including the Bold Slasher and the Turkish Knight. If one of St. George's enemies is wounded, the Doctor steps in to offer his services. Sometimes the Devil and the Fat Lady participate.

Beginning on December 12, the Christmas Men (13 mischievous Santas who descend from Gryla the Ogre) visit homes throughout **Iceland**. One of the Santas makes the rounds each night until December 25. No one ever sees the Christmas Men, but you know when they've been to your home. Some leave gifts. Others signal their arrival by slamming a door or blowing out a candle.

Children in **Belgium** and **Holland** receive their gifts on St. Nicholas Day (December 7). They leave their wooden shoes out before they go to sleep and hope for St. Nick's generosity.

During Advent (the four weeks before Christmas Day), people in **Twente, Holland** blow horns to chase away the evil spirits of winter. They make the horns themselves, using one-year-old elder saplings.

The three Thursday evenings before Christmas in **Germany** are known as the Knocking Nights. Children dress in masks and go from door to door reciting rhymes and ringing cowbells in an effort to drive away evil spirits (and to be rewarded with candy or coins).

The Christmas season in **Rome** begins on December 8, when men from the Roman Fire Department climb a ladder to put a fresh garland on the statue of the Virgin Mary at the top of Piazza di Spagna's high obelisk.

During the Christmas season, skinny Italian Santas and Befanas (gift-bearing witches) hang out in the Piazza Navona. Here, too, you'll find shepherds playing *Tu Scendi Dalle Stelle*, Italy's only Christmas carol, on their *zampogna* (bagpipes).

Many Roman Christmas traditions involve eating. Before or after going to midnight mass, Romans sit down to *il cenone*, a meatless feast. The feast is finished off with the traditional Christmas cakes: *panettone* and *pandoro*. On Christmas Day is *il pranzo di Natale*, the Christmas lunch.

On Christmas Eve in **Spain** (known as the Night of Good Tidings), everyone attends mass, which ends at midnight when, according to scriptures, the cock crowed for the first time on the eve of Christ's birth. (The cock crowed again at 3 a.m. and 6 a.m.)

One of the most unusual Spanish Christmas traditions is the Olentzero, which re-enacts the story of a charcoal burner who came down from the mountains to tell of Christ's birth. During the re-enactment in Navarre, the charcoal burner of the Olentzero is carried shoulder-high through town on Christmas Eve.

On Christmas Eve in **Sweden**, the children aren't visited by Santa Claus (despite the country's proximity to the North Pole). Instead, Swedish children await the Yule Goat (Julbock). Sometime during the evening's festivities, the Yule Goat pushes open the front door and throws in his presents.

Christmas Eve in **France** is celebrated with the *reveillon*, a traditional meal that follows midnight mass.

December 31: New Year's Eve

Celebrating the end of a year is perhaps the world's oldest custom. Today we blow horns and ring bells at the strike of midnight to welcome the new year. Centuries ago, people rang bells and blew horns on New Year's Eve to frighten away the devils of the old year and to keep them from following into the new one.

New Year's Eve in **Rome** is a colorful and frenzied affair. Everyone dresses in new red underwear, a practice the Romans believe brings prosperity, happiness, and good luck. At midnight the skies explode with fireworks—and garbage. The people heave all their broken, useless debris out the windows. You'll see old clothes and burned pots as well as damaged furniture and toilets flying into the streets.

In **Denmark**, people send out the old year by smashing crockery against doors. Celebrants in **Spain** must eat 12 grapes from a bunch between the first and last tolls of the midnight bells. If they are successful, they are assured a prosperous new year. In the **German** village of Oberammergau, a "star singer" carrying an illuminated star on a pole leads a procession through town on New Year's Eve.

On New Year's Eve in **Greece** not only children but grownups as well go from house to house singing the *Kalanda*, a song of good wishes. On the Greek island of Hios, caroling sailors parade through the streets with ship models.

The tradition of First Footing remains very important in some European countries, including Scotland. The appearance and character of the first person to enter your house after midnight on New Year's Eve foretells your fortune for the coming year. Most families go to some lengths to make sure a tall, dark, and trustworthy person is the first to step over their thresholds.

If you'd prefer a more cultural evening on New Year's Eve, try **Vienna, Austria.** Here, Europe's elite brings in the new year by attending a performance of *Die Fledermaus*.

Chapter 4

Address Book

Following is a list of organizations that may be able to help you plan your next trip to Europe. Included are national tourist boards, embassies, international airlines and cruise lines, national railroads that offer discount passes, and car rental agencies with offices in Europe. The addresses and telephone numbers listed with each are for the main offices. Check the Yellow Pages of your local telephone directory for the offices nearest you.

NATIONAL TOURIST BOARDS

Andorran Bureau for Tourism, *1923 W. Irving Park, Chicago, IL 60613; (312)472-7660.*

Austrian National Tourist Office, *500 Fifth Ave., New York, NY 10110; (212)944-6880.*

Belgian National Tourist Office, *745 Fifth Ave., New York, NY 10151; (212)758-8130.*

British Tourist Authority, *40 W. 57th St., New York, NY 10019; (212)581-4708.*

Bulgarian Tourist Office (Balkantourist), *161 E. 86th St., New York, NY 10028; (212)722-1110.*

Cyprus Tourism Organization, *13 E. 40th St., New York, NY 10016; (212)213-9100.*

Czechoslovakian Travel Bureau (CEDOK), *10 E. 40th St., New York, NY 10016; (212)689-9720.*

French Government Tourist Office, *610 Fifth Ave., New York, NY 10020; (212)757-1125.*

German Tourist Office, *747 Third Ave., New York, NY 10017; (212)308-3300.*

Greek National Tourist Organization, *645 Fifth Ave., New*

York, NY 10022; (212)421-5777.

Hungarian Travel Bureau (IBUSZ), *630 Fifth Ave., New York, NY 10111; (212)582-7412.*

Irish Tourist Board, *757 Third Ave., New York, NY 10017; (212)418-0800.*

Italian Government Travel Office, *630 Fifth Ave., New York, NY 10111; (212)245-4822.*

Luxembourg National Tourist Office, *801 Second Ave., New York, NY 10017; (212)370-9850.*

Monaco Government Tourist Office, *845 Third Ave., New York, NY 10022; (212)759-5227.*

Netherlands National Tourist Office, *355 Lexington Ave., 21st Floor, New York, NY 10017; (212)370-7360.*

Polish National Tourist Office (Poloris), *500 Fifth Ave., New York, NY 10110; (212)391-0844.*

Portuguese National Tourist Office, *548 Fifth Ave., New York, NY 10036; (212)354-4403.*

Romanian National Tourist Office, *573 Third Ave., New York, NY 10016; (212)697-6971.*

Scandinavian National Tourist Offices (Denmark, Finland, Iceland, Norway, and Sweden), *655 Third Ave., New York, NY 10017; (212)949-2333.*

Spanish National Tourist Office, *665 Fifth Ave., New York, NY 10022; (212)759-8822.*

Swiss National Tourist Office, *608 Fifth Ave., New York, NY 10020; (212)757-5944.*

Turkish Government Tourism and Information Office, *821 United Nations Plaza, New York, NY 10017; (212)687-2194.*

U.S.S.R. (Intourist), *630 Fifth Ave., Suite 280, New York, NY 10111; (212)757-3884.*

Yugoslav State Tourist Office, *630 Fifth Ave., New York, NY 10111; (212)757-2801.*

EMBASSIES

Embassy of Austria, *2343 Massachusetts Ave. N.W., Washington, DC; 20008; (202)483-4474.*

Embassy of Cyprus, *2211 R St. N.W., Washington, DC 20008;*

(202)462-5772.

Embassy of Czechoslovakia, *3900 Linnean Ave. N.W., Washington, DC; 20008; (202)363-6315; visa section, (202)363-6308* (mornings only).

Embassy of Denmark, *3200 Whitehaven St. N.W., Washington, DC 20008; (202)234-4300.*

Embassy of East Germany, *1717 Massachusetts Ave. N.W., Washington, DC 20036; (202)232-3134.*

Embassy of Finland, *3216 New Mexico Ave. N.W., Washington, DC 20016; (202)363-2430.*

Embassy of France, *4101 Reservoir Rd. N.W., Washington, DC 20007; (202)944-6000.*

Embassy of German Federal Republic, *4645 Reservoir Road N.W., Washington, DC 20007; (202)298-4000;* visa section, *(202)298-4350.*

Embassy of Greece, *2211 Massachusetts Ave. N.W., Washington, DC 20008; (202)667-3168.*

Embassy of the Hungarian Peoples's Republic, *3910 Shoemaker St. N.W., Washington, DC 20008; (202)362-6730;* visa section, *(202)362-6769.*

Embassy of Iceland, *2022 Connecticut Ave. N.W., Washington, DC 20008, (202)265-6653.*

Embassy of Ireland, *2234 Massachusetts Ave. N.W., Washington, DC 20008; (202)462-3939.*

Embassy of Italy, *1601 Fuller St. N.W., Washington, DC 20009; (202)328-5500.*

Embassy of Luxembourg, *2200 Massachusetts Ave. N.W., Washington, DC 20008; (202)265-4171.*

Embassy of Monaco, contact the Embassy of France, *address above.*

Embassy of the Netherlands, *4200 Linnean Ave. N.W., Washington, DC 20008; (202)244-5300.*

Embassy of Norway, *2720 34th St. N.W., Washington, DC 20008; (202)333-6000.*

Embassy of Poland, *2640 16th St. N.W., Washington, DC 20009; (202)234-3800.*

Embassy of Portugal, *2125 Kalorama Road N.W., Washington,*

DC 20008; (202)328-8610.

Embassy of Romania, *1607 23rd St. N.W., Washington, DC 20008; (202)232-4747.*

Embassy of Spain, *2700 15th St. N.W., Washington, DC 20009; (202)265-0190.*

Embassy of Sweden, *600 New Hampshire Ave. N.W., Suite 1200, Washington, DC 20037; (202)944-5600.*

Embassy of Switzerland, *2900 Cathedral Ave. N.W., Washington, DC 20008; (202)745-7900;* tourist information, *(202)745-7958;* visa section, *(202)745-7937.*

Embassy of Turkey, *2523 Massachusetts Ave. N.W., Washington, DC 20008; (202)483-5366.*

Embassy of U.S.S.R., *1125 16th St. N.W., Washington, DC 20036; (202)628-7551.*

Embassy of Yugoslavia, *2410 California St. N.W., Washington, DC 20008; (202)462-6566.*

INTERNATIONAL AIRLINES

Aer Lingus, *(800)223-6537;* flies to England and Ireland.

Air France, *(800)237-2747;* flies to Austria, England, France, Italy, Monaco, and Poland.

Air Portugal, *(800)221-7370* or *(800)221-7370;* flies to Portugal.

ALIA Royal Jordanian Airlines, *(800)223-0470;* flies to Austria and the Netherlands.

Alitalia, *(800)223-5730;* flies to Italy.

American Trans Air, *(800)428-3300* or *(317)247-4000;* flies to Denmark, England, France, Germany, Greece, Ireland, and Italy.

Balair, *(212)581-3411;* flies to Switzerland.

British Airways, *(800)247-9297;* flies to London and Manchester, England.

British Caledonian Airways, *(800)231-0270;* flies to Britain.

Condor, *(312)951-0005;* flies to Frankfurt, Germany.

Continental Airlines, *(800)231-0856;* flies to England and France.

Council Charter, *(800)223-7402* or *(212)661-0311;* flies to Belgium, Denmark, England, France, Holland, Italy, Spain, and

Switzerland.

Czechoslovak Airlines CSA, *(800)223-2365;* flies to Czechoslovakia, East Germany, Hungary, Poland, Romania, and the U.S.S.R.

Delta, *(800)221-1212;* flies to England, France, and Germany.

Finnair, *(800)223-5700;* flies to Finland.

Highland Express, *(800)533-7737* or *(212)983-6760;* flies to England and Scotland.

Iberia, *(800)221-9741;* flies to Spain.

Icelandair, *(800)223-5500;* flies to England, France, Germany, Luxembourg, the Scandinavian countries, and Scotland.

KLM Royal Dutch Lines, *(800)556-9000;* flies to Germany and the Netherlands.

LOT Polish Airlines, *(800)223-0593* or *(212)869-1074;* flies to Poland.

LTU German Lines, *(800)421-5842;* flies to Germany.

Lufthansa German Airlines, *(800)645-3880;* flies to Austria, Germany, Greece, Hungary, Poland, and Yugoslavia.

Martinair, *(516)627-8711* or *(800)847-6677;* flies to the Netherlands.

Northwest Orient, *(800)447-4747,* flies to Denmark, England, Germany, Ireland, Norway, Scotland, and Sweden.

Olympic Airways, *(800)223-1226;* flies to Greece.

Pan Am, *(800)221-1111;* flies to Austria, Belgium, Czechoslovakia, Denmark, Finland, Greece, Hungary, Italy, Norway, Poland, Sweden, Switzerland, the Netherlands, the U.S.S.R., and Yugoslavia.

Rich Airways, *(305)871-5113;* flies to France.

Sabena Airlines, *(516)466-6100;* flies to Austria, Belgium, Denmark, Finland, France, Germany, Greece, Hungary, Ireland, Italy, Luxembourg, Norway, Portugal, Spain, Sweden, Switzerland, and the Netherlands.

Scanair, *(305)932-1231* or *(800)358-7827;* flies to Norway and Sweden (out of Ft. Lauderdale, Florida only).

Scandinavian Airlines, *(800)221-2350;* flies to the Scandinavian countries.

Spantax Airlines, *(212)582-8257;* flies to Spain.
Swissair, *(718)990-4500* or *(800)221-4750;* flies to Switzerland.
Tarom, *(212)687-6013/4;* flies to Austria and Romania.
Tower Air, *(800)824-5083;* flies to Greece and Spain.
TWA, *(800)438-2929* or *(301)338-1156;* flies to Austria,
England, France, Germany, and Spain.
UTA French Airlines, *(800)282-4484;* flies to France and
Monaco.
Yugoslav Airlines; *(800)752-6528;* flies to Greece, the U.S.S.R.,
and Yugoslavia.

CRUISE LINES

Astor Cruises (Interworld Tours), *(800)845-6622* or *(800)221-3882.*
Chandris Fantasy Cruise Lines, *(800)223-0848.*
Costa Cruises, *(800)447-6877* or *(800)462-6782.*
Cruise International, *(800)647-0009.*
Cruise World, *(800)874-3220.*
Cunard Cruise Lines, *(800)528-6273* or *(305)266-8705.*
Epirotiki Lines Inc., *(800)221-2470.*
Exprinter Cruises, *(800)221-1666.*
German Rhine Line, *(914)948-3600* (American representative).
Hellenic Mediterranean Lines, *(415)989-7434* or *(800)257-7055.*
Holland America Line, *(800)626-9900.*
International Cruise Center, *(800)221-3254.*
K Lines Hellenic Cruises, *(800)223-7880.*
Ocean Cruise Lines, *(800)556-8850.*
Princess Cruises, *(800)344-2626.*
Regency Cruises, *(212)972-4774.*
Royal Cruise Line, *(800)227-5628* or *(800)622-0538.*
Royal Viking Line, *(800)346-8000.*
Salen Lindblad Cruising, *(800)223-5688.*
Spur of the Moment Cruises, *(800)343-1991.*
Sun Line Cruises, *(800)872-6400* or *(800)468-6400.*

CAR RENTAL AGENCIES

American International Rent-A-Car, *(800)527-0202.*
Auto Europe, *(800)223-5555* or *(800)342-5205.*
Avis Rent-A-Car, *(800)331-2112.*
Budget Rent-A-Car, *(800)527-0700.*
Dollar Rent-A-Car, *(800)421-6868.*
Europe by Car, *(800)223-1516* or *(212)581-3044.*
Foremost Euro-Car, *(800)423-3111* or *(800)272-3299.*
Kemwell, *(800)468-0468.*
The Cortell Group, *(800)223-6626* or *(800)442-4481.*
Wheels International Rent-A-Car, *(800)663-8888.*

NATIONAL RAILROADS

Austrian Railroads, *500 Fifth Ave., New York, NY 10110;
(212)944-6880.*
Belgian National Railroads, *745 Fifth Ave., New York, NY
10151; (212)758-8130.*
BritRail Travel International, *630 Third Ave., New York, NY
10017; (212)599-5400.*
European Rail, *918 16th St., Washington, DC 20006; (202)659-
9581*
French National Railroads, *610 Fifth Ave., New York, NY
10020; (212)582-2110;* includes France, Luxembourg, Monaco,
and Spain.
German Federal Railroads, *747 Third Ave., New York, NY
10017; (212)308-3106.*
Italian State Railroads, *666 Fifth Ave., New York, NY 10019;
(212)397-2667.*
Swiss Federal Railroads, *608 Fifth Ave., New York, NY 10020;
(212)757-5944.*

Bibliography

Earthstepper Manual, Marian Cooper, Agora Books, 824 E. Baltimore St., Baltimore, MD, 1986.

European Customs and Manners, Nancy L. Braganti and Elizabeth Devine, Meadowbrook Books, 18318 Minnetonka Blvd., Deephaven, MN 55391, 1984.

Herald Tribune Guide to Business Travel and Entertainment in Europe, Peter Graham, An Owl Book, Holt, Rinehart, and Winston, New York, NY 1984.

Hiking and Walking Guide to Europe, Arthur Howcroft and Richard Sale, Passport Books, 4255 W. Touhy Ave., Lincolnwood, IL 60646, 1984.

How To Europe, The Complete Travelers' Handbook, John Bermont, Murphy and Broad Publishing Company, 425 30th St., P.O. Box 3208, Newport Beach, CA 92663, 1984.

Money Saving Secrets of Smart Airline Travelers, Capt. Richard A. Bodner, Betterway Publications Inc., White Hall, VA 22987, 1986.

Safety and Health Abroad, John A. Giordano and Mary Shaughnessy Shea, Datafax Corporation, Minneapolis, MN, 1985.

The Frequent Flyer Guide, Kriss Hammond, 1220 Third St., Spearfish, SD 57783, 1987.

The New York Times Practical Traveler, Paul Grimes, Times Books, New York, NY 1985.

The Travel and Vacation Discount Guide, Paige Palmer, Pilot Industries Inc., 103 Cooper St., Babylon, NY 11702, 1987.

The World's Best, Marian Cooper, Agora Books, 824 E. Baltimore St., Baltimore, MD 21202, 1986.

Travelers' Almanac, the International Guide, Bill Munster, 6900 Santa Monica Blvd., Los Angeles, CA 90038, distributed by Rand McNally and Company, Chicago, New York, San Francisco, 1985.

Acknowledgements

This book was a daunting task. Without the many writers, researchers, and editors who helped, it wouldn't have been possible. My gratitude goes especially to Janet Schamehorn, who helped me with so many easily forgotten details. I am grateful, too, to Elizabeth Philip, the consulting editor. Then there are the many interns who helped: Gary Almes, Ellen Chang, Lee Diemer, Michael Meresman, Eve Oishi, Natalie Shelpuk, and Loren Fox.

And last, but by no means least, thanks are due the copy editors, Kathie Peddicord and Brenda Greene, who spent hours perusing my manuscripts. Kathy Murphy kept us on schedule—a difficult task, to say the least. Denise Plowman kept the copy rolling. And Becky Mangus made it all look pretty in the end.

—*Marian Cooper*